Charles Way
Three Plays

Seren Drama

The View from Row G: Dannie Abse
Three Plays: Gwyn Thomas
Three Plays: Edward Thomas

Charles Way
Three Plays

Dead Man's Hat
Paradise Drive
In the Bleak Midwinter

Edited by Brian Mitchell

seren

seren
is the book imprint of
Poetry Wales Press Ltd.
First Floor, 2 Wyndham Street
Bridgend, Mid Glamorgan
Wales, CF31 1EF

British Library Cataloguing In Publication Data:

Way, Charles
Three Plays
I. Title
822.914

ISBN: 1-85411-114-0

The publisher acknowledges the financial assistance of the Arts Council of Wales.
With special thanks to the Drama Section.

Cover: Andy Dark

Printed by WBC Book Manufacturers Ltd, Bridgend

Contents

For Liz.

Introduction

The three plays in this volume were written to be toured to small or middle scale venues. This means not only the smaller theatres but village halls and community centres, to audiences who might not in general terms be regular theatre-goers. It is within this world of touring theatre with all its frustrations and joys that I have been nurtured as a playwright. Naturally it has affected my way of telling stories, which is essentially what I do. In a theatre with a thick carpet you can't hear the audience leaving, but in the village hall there is no escaping the audience or their reaction to the play. The situation demands therefore that the story is told with great economy and clarity of purpose. It's been my aim to achieve this without loss in regard to character motivation and development.

There is always, in any good play, the story beneath the story. This relates to why the writer became a writer in the first place and why he or she wants to tell this particular tale. It is an awareness of this, at whatever level, which ties an audience into a play, and this brings me to the three plays here.

Dead Man's Hat is a psychological Western based on the simple notion of turning the premise of the film *Shane* on its head. A gunslinger arrives at a small Wyoming farmstead and gets caught up in the battle between corporate business (cattle ranching) and individual rights (farming). In *Shane* the gunslinger is at best a good man trying to go straight. In *Dead Man's Hat* the gunslinger is your run of the mill, voice in the head, all-American psychopath, intent on destroying the very thing he wants most, a family. He is attractive but deadly and embodies the ambivalence I feel towards America and its culture, which as a child was a good deal closer to me than the North of England.

INTRODUCTION

The Western has traditionally been a genre which critics have ignored or scorned but audiences enjoy. There are of course more than a fistful of silly Westerns, but the best are metaphors, and achieve a tragic grandeur akin to Greek drama. *Dead Man's Hat* reaches out in that direction.

The other two plays, *In The Bleak Midwinter* and *Paradise Drive,* were written with and for Hijinx Theatre in Cardiff with whom I have been able to develop an invigorating partnership. Both plays were developed to scenario form and then offered to the actors to stimulate improvisation. During this process I rarely write down what the actors say but use the improvisations to discover emotional truths, characters, images and theatre moments. Without the input of the director and actors in this process these two plays would not have become what they are. That the plays are still highly personal, in that only one person could have written them, is a credit to the mature working process Hijinx Theatre had developed and which due to inadequate funding is now under threat.

In The Bleak Midwinter is a play which harnesses the energy and fun of the nativity story as told in medieval mystery plays. The story beneath the story here is my personal struggle with religion embodied in the clash between Miriam, the realist and Zac, the dreamer. I am not a great follower of absolute truths and the play takes three of the great Commandments and gently chips away at them. The great injury religions do is based on the idea that the belief is more important than the people who believe. This unleashes the worst in people and allows for none of the compromise and humanity implicit in the metaphor of Zac and Miriam's marriage.

Paradise Drive is in some ways, the odd play out here in that it is modern and domestic. It tells the story of a family during Mrs Thatcher's ten years in office and charts the effect of the political and moral climate of the 1980's on the lives of its four characters. The play is based on a true incident gleaned form a newspaper article about an artist who committed suicide in the belief that she and her art served no useful purpose. It is a dark play which stimulated wildly opposing critical points of view. Beneath its shadows, however, there lies a conviction that artists are important, that stories, culture, society actually do exist and matter.

I would like to thank the directors Bill Buffery *(Dead Man's Hat)* and Rosamund Hutt *(Paradise Drive,* and *In The Bleak Mid winter)*, for their belief in my work, and for their own talents which brought the plays successfully to the stage and thence to this book. My appreciation also goes to the three musicians, Tom Nordon, Paula Gardiner, and Philip Thomas, whose music added more than I can say and wouldn't a tune say it better anyway; The designers, Meg Surrey and Richard Aylwin, and last, but naturally not least, those bands of actors who tour this country for very little remuneration, but know at least that they are involved in something of value, the telling of a story, told not to one person but to a group. The act of theatre is an act of society, an act of hope.

Charles Way

Dead Man's Hat

Notes to the Original Production

Dead Man's Hat was first performed by the Orchard Theatre Company at the Plough Theatre, Torrington on Thursday 1st October, 1992.

Cast

Kate Watson..Gill Nathanson
Anne Watson................................Andrea Gascoigne
Jim Averill...James Lailey
Clay..Andrew Howard
Frank Dolan.......................................David Plimmer

additional characters:

Young Mr Dickson
Old Mr Dickson
Two killers
A saloon singer
Cullen Masters

The play was originally written for a cast of five, doubling as follows:

Jim Averill + Cullen Masters + Old Mr Dickson
Frank Dolan + Young Mr Dickson

Director...Bill Buffery
Music...Tom Nordon
Stage Manager.....................................Andy Shewan
Set Design..Meg Surrey

Act One

SONG: *[One voice.]*

Of all the mighty nations in the East
or in the West
The glorious Yankee nation is the greatest
and the best
We have room for all creation
and our banner is unfurled
With a general invitation to the people
of the world.

ALL: So come along, come along, make no delay
Come from every nation, come from every way
Our lands they are broad enough, don't be alarmed
For Uncle Sam is rich enough to give us all a farm.

[Guitar continues under the Storytellers.]

STORY-TELLERS: It was a Sunday
In the late Fall of 1935
Johnson County, Wyoming.
Miss Anne Watson, sixty years of age
Sat on the porch of her house
Watching the sun sink slowly in the west,

[One of the Storytellers becomes Anne Watson.]

As a young gentleman from Boston
Rode up to the house on a bicycle.

ANNE: Said he was from some society or other.

DICKSON: The Historical Society of the American West.

ANNE: Wanted to find out about the Valley and the first homesteaders, what we did, what we ate, what songs we sang, everything. Said he wanted the truth. Truth is most folks came out West on empty stomachs. This was their Canaan, the promised land.

SONG: So come along, come along, make no delay
Come from every nation come from every way
Our lands they are broad enough don't be alarmed
Come to the land of Freedom and vote yerself a farm.

ANNE: Once I started talkin' I couldn't stop. I talked till I had no more breath left in me to blow a smoke ring. Even forgot to ask the young man's name.

DICKSON: Dickson — Harold Dickson — at your service.

ANNE: Dickson?

DICKSON: Yes, Ma'am. Miss Watson, the Society will be much impressed by the material you've supplied but I must confess a personal interest in coming to see you today.

[Pause.]

You see I'm trying to find out what happened to my Grandfather, Elias Dickson. He was an actor of sorts, appeared with Buffalo Bill once. I traced his movements to Deadwood City in the Spring of 1892 and then he just seems to have disappeared off the face of the earth. Family never heard of him again. He was heading for Brandonsville and since you lived here so long, I wondered if you had ever heard of a man of that name, Elias Dickson.

[Silence.]

Miss Watson?

ANNE: There's always somethin' else, ain't there?

DICKSON: Ma'am?

ANNE: Man comes up to the house says he wants one thing when he really wants another.

DICKSON: Miss Watson, this is very important to me.

ANNE: Why? Ain't you yerself?

DICKSON: I'd just like to find out what happened to him — that's all.

[Silence.]

ANNE: Look around you, Mr Dickson. Pretty valley, ain't it?

DICKSON: Uh — yes, Ma'am. Garden of Eden.

[She smiles at this.]

ANNE: Over there's Brandonsville.

DICKSON: I came through it.

ANNE: Everything's changed there, railroad came then shops, sidewalks, streetlamps. Was a time when it was no more than four frame buildings with a muddy streak before it. Out here there was nothin', 'cept this house stickin' out of the prairie like... *[she shakes her head]*...like some sort o' mistake.

[Her mind drifts for a moment.]

I got time these days to sit out here an' go back over things, Mr Dickson. Each time I go back over things it seems, I don't know how to say it — like it gets farther away — like we was all just folks in a dime novel, once upon a time, you know what I'm sayin'?

DICKSON: Yes, Ma'am.

ANNE: I'm sayin' I can only tell what I recall an' what I pieced together over the years an' that ain't the same as the truth.

DICKSON: Yes, Ma'am.

ANNE: Regular Yes Ma'am — ain't ya?

DICKSON: Ye... *[he bites his lip]* Excuse me. You start as you think fit — anyway — once upon a time...

ANNE: There was a gunman called Cullen Masters. You heard of him?

DICKSON: Yes, Ma'am. He's famous.

ANNE: I never saw him myself but I know pretty much what he looked like — he used to dress all in black, with one of them thin black ties.

[Enter Cullen Masters.]

He wore one gun, 'cos one was enough. A Colt 45 Single Action Peacemaker.

[Images of the past which begin here, should have a filmic quality, creating pictures for the audience which are familiar. At the beginning and ends of key scenes the images could be held, almost as if the camera has stopped, to capture the mythic quality of the story, and as a particularly sharp memory of Anne's.]

DICKSON: Is there some connection between my Grandfather and Cullen Masters?

ANNE: I'm gettin' to it. About a hundred mile from here, guess it was '92, like you say, Cullen Masters held a necktie party.

[Masters throws a lynching rope.]

The chief guest was a man called Clay.

[Clay enters and puts his neck in the noose.]

DICKSON: *[writing in his notebook]* Clay.

ANNE: Ain't I speakin' clear enough for ya?

DICKSON: Yes, Ma'am.

ANNE: Masters stood Clay on the box an' told him to sing.

[The action in the past continues.]

CLAY: Glory, Glory, Hallelujah
Glory, Glory, Hallelujah
His truth is marching on.

[Cullen Masters joins in the last phrase.]

MASTERS: Amen.

[Masters puts on his hat.]

CLAY: Why you doin' this, Masters? I oughta know, 'cos when I reach the other side the Lord is sure to ask.

MASTERS: Well, I'll tell ya.

CLAY: I'd be grateful.

MASTERS: You give me a bad feelin', Clay.

CLAY: Is that it? Is that all I done?

MASTERS: I'm a God fearin' man, Clay.

CLAY: I know that.

MASTERS: Every killin' I done, I done the right way an' in his name. But not you —

CLAY: Me? What did I do?

MASTERS: We ain't barbarians, Clay. There's meanin' in the way we do things.

CLAY: Yeah? What's the meaning of this?

MASTERS: This means you can't ride with my outfit no more.

CLAY: Where you goin'? Ain't ya goin' to kick the box now? A man could do some sufferin' here.

MASTERS: If you wanna jump, go ahead an' jump.

[Masters moves away.]

CLAY: Masters? Masters? Shit. I'll see you in Hell! Shit!

ANNE: Clay wasn't the jumpin' kind — he stood on that box for near two days when who should happen along, out of the wilderness, but a mild mannered man carryin' a carpet bag.

[The actor playing Masters, in view of the audience, becomes Dickson's Grandfather.]

OLD DICKSON: Oh my God — my dear God — in heaven. Alright — its alright — I'm here — Oh my God.

ANNE: An' he cut Clay down. Would've saved us all some heartache if he'd let him swing, but he didn't, he cut him down, brought him back from the dead.

[Mr Dickson has cut Clay down. The lights have faded a little. The new scene is Clay and Dickson round a campfire.]

ANNE: Clay and — your Mr Dickson rode together for a couple of days — they set up camp about eighty mile from here. Up there in the hills behind us. [*Clay plays harmonica*]

CLAY: That's a fine hat, Mr Dickson.

DICKSON: I had it made special for my profession. Do you hear something?

CLAY: No.

DICKSON: Maybe those fellers who lynched you will come back?

CLAY: What they want to come back fer? I'm dead, ain't I?

[Dickson tries to pour himself a coffee but his hands are shaking and he spills it.]

CLAY: Where you headed, Mr Dickson?

DICKSON: *[shrugs]* I heard some fellers have found some gold up in the Yukon. Great big bucketfuls. I might try my luck too.

[He goes to the edge of the fire's light and looks out.]

CLAY: Sit down, Mr Dickson. Yer makin' the horses nervous.

DICKSON: It's a great mystery to me, Mr Clay, why one man believes he has the right to kill another. The coyotes have more respect for their own kind. What reason did your would be lynch mob give?

CLAY: No reason. No reason at all.

DICKSON: That's my point. That's what I'm talking about, Mr Clay. Respect for life. Lucky for you I happened along.

CLAY: I'm grateful.

DICKSON: Your probably wondering what I'm doing out here in the wilderness.

[Silence.]

DICKSON: Like yourself, I am a man of adventure.

[Pause.]

DICKSON: Naturally I'm a law abiding citizen, but recently found myself in difficulties in Deadwood City, while in pursuit of an honest dollar.

[He gives Clay a book.]

CLAY: I don't read.

DICKSON: *Deadwood Dick and the White Squaw.* I gather from your expression you've never heard of Deadwood Dick.

CLAY: No sir.

DICKSON: He's a rare man, Mr Clay, a rare man. Buffalo Bill may kill a hundred Apaches but Deadwood Dick kills a hundred more, single handed. He's what we call a fictional character. The readers back East have come to believe that Deadwood Dick is real — that he's out here riding the plains, killing Indians and rescuing white girls. It makes their lives exciting and yet safe.

[Pause.]

They'd like to meet him if they could — travel West to do so, to thank him and to press a coin into his "gunsmooth palm". Wouldn't you like to meet him, Mr Clay?

CLAY: Sure. He's a rare man.

[Dickson pulls out a buckskin suit and holds it up against himself.]

DICKSON: Presenting Mr Deadwood Dick — you see.

CLAY: You?

DICKSON: Indeed — here's my picture. That's me. I had it taken for the newspapers. Publicity. I went to Dodge an' there were ladies from New York pleased as pie to see me in person. Same all over and eventually I arrived in Deadwood. A scum-ridden nest of whores and thieves but still an appropriate place for my line of work. However I soon discovered there were two other Deadwood Dicks in Deadwood. They had a fight and the winner came looking for me. So here I am in the middle of nowhere in your esteemed company.

CLAY: Truly, Mr Dickson — you are a man of adventure.

DICKSON: *[laughs]* And — and enterprise.... Mr Clay, we will probably part company in the morning and I was wondering if you would like to take advantage of a special offer, which due to my thespian connections I alone am privvy to. It's hair lotion — very fine lotion — for the hair. Very fine indeed.

CLAY: *[takes it]* Thank you, Mr Dickson.

[He puts it away.]

DICKSON: That's, that's, that's totally free of course.

CLAY: I'm obliged.

DICKSON: There's someone out there — I know it. *[he stands]* Who's there? Come out and show yourself. *[Clay takes out his gun]* My companion and I are armed and at the ready. So come out.

[Clay shoots Dickson once in the back. He then picks up the white hat and puts it on.]

ANNE: Most of it Clay told me himself — not directly you understand — bit by bit, little by little.

YOUNG DICKSON: He just shot him? In cold blood?

[She nods.]

What happened to this man Clay? Was he brought to justice? Well, was he?

[She gives him a sharp look. Silence.]

Miss Watson. I have to know.

ANNE: Why? You gettin' revengeful already?

YOUNG DICKSON: I didn't mean to offend you. *[pause]* I've come a long way, Miss Watson. Been searchin' for years, and somehow I still don't feel like I found him — not until I know what happened to this — this man Clay.

ANNE: What happened to Clay is what happened to me.

YOUNG DICKSON: I understand —

ANNE: I doubt it. *[silence]* Anyways yer Grandpa ain't out of the story yet.

YOUNG DICKSON: But you said he was killed...

ANNE: I'll get there, Mr Dickson. *[pause]* Clay rode into our lives one fine spring morning in 1892. I was seventeen.

SONG: *[One voice.]*

To the West
To the West
To the land of the free.

ANNE: I could see him plain, just another stray horseman riding up the road toward the cluster of frame buildings that was Brandonsville.

SONG: Where the mighty Missouri
Rolls down to the sea.

ANNE: But he didn't stop in the town. He kept coming steadily until he reached the fork half a mile below our place. He hesitated briefly then made his choice.

[Enter Clay.]

SONG: Where the young may exalt
And the aged may rest
Away far away
In the land of the West.

[We have now slipped back in time. Clay stands wearing the white hat and carrying the carpet bag that he stole from Dickson. Anne, during the last section of the song, has become seventeen years old.]

[Anne faces Clay with a gun.]

CLAY: Mornin'.

ANNE: What do you want?

CLAY: Is your Pa here?

ANNE: He's here.

[Clay looks around.]

I said he's here.

CLAY: Is he very thin?

ANNE: He's out in the fields — one shot of this an' he'll come runnin'.

CLAY: Yer Ma then.

ANNE: She's in town pickin' up some stores but she'll be back soon.

CLAY: That's a big gun, Miss...

ANNE: I know what it is.

CLAY: 50 Calibre Sharps...

ANNE: I said I know what it is.

[Silence.]

CLAY: You're awful wire-edged.

ANNE: You work for Quinell?

CLAY: Who's he?

ANNE: Don't lie to me.

CLAY: Be a sin to lie to you. *[silence]* Mind if I lead my horse to water?

ANNE: She's found it. You stay put...please.

CLAY: I just want to water my horse, maybe rest up a couple o' days.

ANNE: You'll have to ask Ma. *[she lowers the gun]* You a cowhand?

CLAY: Have been. What's yer name?

ANNE: A...What's yours?

CLAY: Clay.

ANNE: Watched you comin' up the trail three mile or more. Never figured you'd stop here. Do you want some coffee?

CLAY: Yes, Miss — thank you.

ANNE: Jim — Jim. *[she bangs the metal triangle]*

CLAY: He ain't yer real Pa then?

ANNE: No. *[silence]* There's a wagon comin'. You can speak to Ma about stayin' over.

[We hear sound of hooves, light rises on Anne's mother Kate on front of a wagon, we hear the sound of the wagon and see Kate pushing the horses on with reins and vocal power. Music could accompany this image. Kate has to fight the horses and she pushes them on with cruel glee then pulls them up fast. She stares across at Clay without expression then gets off the wagon.]

CLAY: I didn't see who you was racin' against but it seems you left 'em a long ways back.

ANNE: Name's Clay.

CLAY: Ma'am.

ANNE: He stopped by lookin' for a place to water and rest up for a while.

[Kate begins to unload the wagon.]

CLAY: Fine lookin' place you got here, Mrs...

ANNE: Watson.

CLAY: All I seed for a hundred miles was sod houses an' then all of a sudden here's yours, two storeys high all made of wood an' painted too. Why it hardly looks like a farm at all.

KATE: Well, it's a farm now make no mistake, Mister...

ANNE: Clay.

KATE: Is that all?

CLAY: *[shrugs]* Call me Clay an' I'll come runnin'.

KATE: Where you from?

CLAY: Texas. Ate dust behind a trail herd most of the way.

KATE: A man comes into a place, asks for water, his horse dyin' on its feet, bin ridin' hard for a couple of days or more. We don't know who he is or what he's ridin' from.

ANNE: He just wants...

KATE: He can speak can't he?

[Jim enters.]

CLAY: I just need some time, Mrs Watson, some fair, honest to God time. That's all — an' I'll pay for it.

JIM: You don't have to pay, Mister. Not for plain good manners anyhow.

KATE: Jim...

JIM: We haven't turned a soul away yet an' we won't start today. That's what Quinell wants — get us acting like we're under siege. Well I won't, because I'm not.

ANNE: His name's Clay.

JIM: Where you headed, Clay?

CLAY: I hear some fellers found gold up in the Yukon — great big bucketfuls.

JIM: Gold? We know all about gold, don't we Kate?

[Kate spits out her baccy in disgust.]

CLAY: You went prospectin'?

JIM: Bodie, California — had no luck at all.

KATE: Yeah — that's where he met me.

[Jim laughs.]

JIM: Name's Averill — Jim Averill. *[they shake hands]* You can sleep in...

KATE: In the lean-to.

CLAY: That's where I'm best — an' if anyone comes by I'll bark as loud as I can.

ANNE: Ma — Jim. They're comin' again. They're comin' again.

[Kate goes to pick up the gun.]

JIM: Kate, we'll talk to them.

KATE: You talk, Jim, you're good at it. There's too many —

JIM: Damn them.

[Music which conveys the drama of a group of cowboys pulling up the fences that Jim has been laying. A light hits Anne.]

ANNE: The cowboys rode across the ford at speed
Pushing their mustangs on with wild glee
Hollerin' and whoopin' as they come.

[We hear this behind her speech.]

An' I can see them across the years
Caught in the moment
With the sun and the water rising up
From the ford all about them
And they ride with an easiness
Born of long days on the trail.
The whole movement of men an' horses,
Bedrolls and lariats, slickers an' guns
Graceful an' dangerous an' excitin'.

SONG: The Cowboys
The Cowboys
They wear their hats with pride
For forty years
They ruled the range
Now they're fighting to survive
'Cos the homesteader came
And he never seems to tire
Of driving in the fences
An' puttin' up the wire
But it won't be long
The cowboys proclaim

Before you hear them singing
On the prairie again
Whoopee ti — yi — yo
Whoopee ti — yi — yo...

ANNE: They swung the catch ropes
Round their hats on to our posts
An' pulled 'em out like old men's teeth.
An all the time their horses
Trampled the potatoes, the alfalfa
And the new corn,
And there was nothing to be done
But stare at the ugliness of their doin'.
They yelled some obscenities
Across the valley floor
An hightailed it out
Leavin' nothin' but hard work behind 'em
And laughin' as they go.

[Sound of hooves and whooping and yelling fading into silence. Jim, Anne and Kate look dejectedly out.]

JIM: This is our land, you hear me, John Quinell — our land. *[silence]* Five days work, Kate, destroyed in five minutes.

[Jim picks up a long-handled mallet.]

KATE: Do it tomorrow, Jim.

[He goes to the back of the stage and takes up his position ready to work again driving in new posts.]

CLAY: Who were they?

KATE: Cowboys workin' for Quinell, that's his spread across the river. Three thousand acres of it — but it don't seem to be enough.

CLAY: They sure are bold about their business.

KATE: That's the fifth time.

CLAY: Well, Ma'am. That ain't right. That ain't right at all.

[Clay joins Jim and they face each other, each holding a long-handled mallet.]

JIM: They're watching us, Clay, from across the river, you swing that hammer and you've chosen sides.

[Clay hits the fence post and then the two men work in an easy rhythm.]

SONG: *[Anne.]*

The farmer is the man
The farmer is the man
Lives on credit till the fall
But if you'll only look and see
I think you will agree
That the farmer is the man who feeds them all.

[The song continues as the scene changes to late at night. Clay is in the lean-to playing his harmonica or washing. Anne stands outside waiting and listening. Kate and Jim sit on the porch.]

SONG: *[Kate.]*

When the banker says he's broke
And the merchant's up in smoke
They forget that it's the farmer feeds them all.
It would put them to the test
If the farmer took a rest
Then they'd know that it's the farmer feeds them all.

ALL: *[Refrain.]*

The farmer is the man
The farmer is the man
Lives on credit till the fall;
His pants are wearing thin
His condition it's a sin,
He's forgot that he's the man who feeds them all...

[Kate and Jim listen to Clay's harmonica for a moment. Kate is turned stubbornly away from Jim.]

JIM: Got something on your mind?

KATE: This ain't your place, Jim, you remember that. *[silence]*

JIM: I'm sorry if...

KATE: If I want a man in the lean-to, I'll go out and buy one.

JIM: *[he smiles]* If I offended — I'm sorry. Still, I could use an extra hand right now. Someone to dig potatoes, plant corn, take the cattle to the railhead; someone who'll stand up to Quinell's boys if he has to.

KATE: You don't know him.

JIM: You think I can't judge a man as well as you?

KATE: You only see the best.

JIM: What do you see?

KATE: *[shrugs]* I don't trust a man who won't tell me his name.

JIM: No doubt he has his reasons.

KATE: No doubt about that.

JIM: Every now and then a man needs a clean slate. Who are we to deny him?

KATE: Don't say we — when you mean 'me'.

[Silence.]

JIM: I don't hold myself above you in any way. You know that, Kate. We can settle this dispute with Quinell. All we have to do is show we're not afraid of him. That we're not afraid to be ourselves, to be reasonable and open. We can start by giving Clay a job.

KATE: Maybe it's not worth it anyhow. Look at us. Our hands are red raw an' our bones so dog tired every night we can hardly lift 'em into bed.

JIM: It's worth it. I came out here because you wrote me and told me it was worth it.

KATE: You'd've come out here whatever I told ya. You was broke.

JIM: I came because you invited me, you said you needed someone you could trust. Someone with a vision of what we can build here. I've got that vision.

KATE: So has Quinell.

JIM: I can take whatever Quinell has to offer.

KATE: I asked you out here to run a farm not ride shotgun for me.

JIM: I'm not afraid of Quinell.

KATE: He's getting meaner all the time, an' I don't know how far he'll go to get what he wants.

JIM: What are you saying?

KATE: I'm just saying — I'd — understand if you decided to go back. I ain't meanin' to be offensive neither.

[Silence.]

JIM: You ever heard of Walt Whitman?

KATE: You know I've never heard of him.

JIM: He's a writer. A fine writer, Kate. He wrote some words and I considered them so highly I learnt them by rote.

KATE: It's gettin' late, Jim.

JIM: Listen. *[pause]* "This is what you shall do, love the earth and sun and animals, despise riches. Give alms to everyone that asks. Stand up for the stupid and the crazy — Argue not concerning God. Have patience and indulgence toward the people. Take off your hat to nothing or to any man or number of men."

[Silence.]

I'm not going to take off my hat to John Quinell or any number of his men.

KATE: You an' yer words. I don't despise riches. I ain't givin' alms to every duffer that asks an' as for the stupid and the crazy, I reckon that's us. What's this?

JIM: It's a letter I've written to *Harpers Monthly.* When they publish it, the whole country will know what's going on here. I truly believe the government has no idea.

KATE: This won't do no good, Jim. It'll just make Quinell mad.

JIM: When he's mad enough I'll go and talk with him. Kate, you know what I want? I want to build the kind of place here that — you'd be proud to come back to in a hundred year's time. Think of that. But you and me and Anne aren't enough.

[They listen to Clay's harmonica.]

Every time they pull the fences down it gets a little harder to put them back up, but when Clay and I set to I felt like nothing on earth could stop us.

[Light rises on Clay washing in a bowl and applying the hair lotion he got from Elias Dickson.)

ANNE: I watched him for a while, the way he smoothed out his shirt an' combed his hair. He even had a little mirror. I never saw a man take such care of himself. Round here it's all bib-overalls an' mud.

[Clay catches her arm.]

CLAY: You shouldn't go spyin' on a man.

[He lets her go.]

ANNE: Don't get many visitors.

CLAY: You'd better go before your Ma finds out where you are.

ANNE: I ain't scared of her.

CLAY: Yes ya are.

ANNE: What's this?

CLAY: Lotion for the hair.

[She smells it.]

Kills bugs and attracts women — so the man said.

ANNE: Guess he got that the wrong way 'round. Nice hat.

CLAY: I had it made special.

ANNE: Where? St. Louis — Dodge City — San Francisco?

CLAY: You'd like to see them towns, wouldn't ya?

ANNE: I will. I'm not stayin' here. So. You're from Texas. Got folks down there?

CLAY: Long time ago. My folks is dead. Didn't even have time to put a name to me.

ANNE: I'm sorry.

[He smiles and waits for her to ask.]

ANNE: What happened?

CLAY: I'll tell ya — but ya have to promise not to laugh.

ANNE: I wouldn't laugh about a thing like that.

CLAY: A wall fell on them. There was an earthquake and they was in bed and the wall fell down and killed 'em. That's what I was told.

[Silence.]

ANNE: *[she smiles]* I'm sorry — I'm really sorry.

CLAY: You don't look too sorry.

[She laughs.]

ANNE: God forgive me, I'm sorry, I'm sorry. *[she is convulsed with laughter]*

CLAY: Well — it was a long time ago.

[Kate approaches the lean-to.]

KATE: Clay!

CLAY: Yes, Ma'am.

[Anne hides.]

KATE: May I speak with you?

CLAY: Yes, Ma'am, one minute.

[He puts on his shirt and comes out.]

KATE: Thanks for helpin' out today.

CLAY: You're welcome.

KATE: Ever done any farming, Clay?

CLAY: No.

KATE: It don't matter, neither had we. We hired a couple of fellers last fall but Quinell's men roughed 'em up pretty bad an' they left.

CLAY: You offering me a job?

KATE: A dollar a day, food an' board.

CLAY: I got to admit, Miss Watson. This place puzzles me. I don't know what you got here. You got a strange lookin' house, I never saw a homestead like it. I never saw a homestead with so many cows — it's like a ranch — but then I ain't seen a ranch with so many damned potatoes. Maybe that's why I'm not sure about what kind of job I'm being offered.

KATE: Well, I'll tell ya. What Jim wants is for you to work the cattle, brand 'em, take 'em up to the railhead when the time comes — can you do that?

CLAY: Yes, Ma'am.

KATE: An' what I want is for you to keep Jim alive. Is that clear enough?

CLAY: Yes, Ma'am.

KATE: Like I say a dollar a day. If you don't want the job you can leave in the mornin', before breakfast. *[she exits]*

CLAY: You'd better go.

ANNE: Why? Are you scared of her too?

CLAY: Ain't everybody?

ANNE: Are you goin' to stay?

CLAY: I'm not decided.

ANNE: I'd like you to. *[silence]* You ever bin to San Francisco?

CLAY: *[nods]* Maybe I'll take you one day. *[silence]* You know they got houses down there made of glass, you can see right through 'em as if they wasn't there.

ANNE: Is that the truth?

CLAY: I seen it with my own eyes. I tell ya a fair crowd gathers 'round them houses at bath times.

[She takes umbrage at this and leaves. She walks over to the porch where Jim has nodded off to sleep. She sits with disgruntled force and wakes him. She hears Clay's harmonica.]

JIM: Anne.

ANNE: You ever been to San Francisco?

JIM: No.

ANNE: Clay says there's houses down there made o' glass.

JIM: Yeah? Maybe there is — new things being invented

every day — things that'll make the world an easier place, a better place.

ANNE: Glass houses? Maybe we should find someone else. Someone we know.

JIM: Don't you like him?

ANNE: I want to.

JIM: He's a good man, Anne. Straight out of the great glowing West is our Clay. But don't get to liking him too much, because he'll leave one day the same as he came.

[She gets up to leave.]

JIM: Anne?

ANNE: What?

JIM: I — May we talk?

ANNE: Sure, long as you don't recite nothin'.

JIM: No, I won't recite anything. Cross my heart. I've been thinking, now we've got the place set up, of asking your Ma to marry me. We can make a real family here, you and Kate and me. What do you think?

ANNE: I've heard Ma swear a hundred times she'd never get married to anyone, 'cos all men is bastards.

JIM: *[laughs]* Well — maybe but this is the land of fresh starts isn't it? That's what the paper said, "Make a fresh start in Wyoming, 180 acres ready to plough." *[Anne smiles]* You mope around here looking sour most of the time. It's nice to see you smile.

ANNE: I can smile if I've got a mind to.

JIM: Just a question of catching her at the right moment. *[pause]* Well, I'll push on off to bed. Goodnight.

[Exit Jim. The harmonica falls silent. Anne goes back to the lean-to.]

ANNE: Clay? Clay? — Clay?

[There's no-one inside. She sees the carpet bag and opens it. She takes out two guns with pearl handles. Clay approaches behind her.]

ANNE: I'm sorry. I didn't mean nothin'.

CLAY: I don't want you goin' through my stuff again, you understand?

[She nods. They stand still for a moment in the half light then she walks to him and kisses him. Lights fade.]

[Lights rise — day dawns. Kate enters with breakfast things, as she works she sings gently to herself.]

SONG: *[Kate.]*

Wake up Jacob
Days a breakin'
Peas in the pot
And the hoecake's bakin'.

Early in the mornin'
Almost day
If you don't come soon
Gonna throw it all away.

[Clay faces Kate.]

CLAY: A dollar a day.

[Jim shakes his hand.]

SONG: Wake up Jacob
Bacon in the pan
Coffee in the pot
Get up an get it
Get it while it's hot.

ANNE: Clay turned out to be a good worker an' in a couple of weeks it seemed like he'd always been here. Quinell's men left us alone for a while, guess they had work of their own. The summer was a beauty, an' I was never so happy with all things tendin' my way, but one mornin', as we sat down to breakfast out in the yard, we saw a rider cross the ford and head our way. Ma!

KATE: Stand back there, Clay, an' don't say nothing. Jim — Frank's coming. *[enter Jim]* You keep civil now.

ANNE: He came alright, the way he'd done a hundred times before.

[Enter Frank Dolan, a trail boss in his middle years, wearing the full gear, i.e. chaps, slicker, etc.]

FRANK: Mornin', Kate.

KATE: Frank.

JIM: You've got a nerve riding in here.

KATE: We was just goin' to have some breakfast.

JIM: Are you going to sit down with him?

KATE: Anne, set Frank a place here.

JIM: God damn it, Kate. God damn it!

[Exit Jim.]

KATE: He's a mite upset on account of some fences.

[Anne pours some coffee.]

FRANK: How are you, Anne?

ANNE: I'm fine, Mr Dolan, just fine.

FRANK: That's the truth. She's all growed up.

KATE: Thinks she is anyhow.

[Anne throws a defiant look at her mother and retreats.]

FRANK: Who's he?

KATE: Haven't yer boys told ya — they watched him close enough.

FRANK: They said you had a new hand working for ya but

he won't come into town to introduce himself.

KATE: You leave him alone. You leave everything alone — including our fences.

[Silence.]

FRANK: Kate — you've gotta listen to me — sell to Quinell, he'll give you a fair price, he's a fair man.

KATE: Haven't seen Quinell in quite a while.

FRANK: He's busy. Hell, Kate, he built this house.

KATE: An' I bought it, fair an' square.

FRANK: Do you think he'd a sold it ya, if he knew you was goin' to turn it into a hay barn?

KATE: That's my business.

FRANK: No it ain't! *[pause]* We're too old, Kate, we can't be nothin' else but what we are.

KATE: You got anything to say or you just blowin' hard the same as usual?

FRANK: What are you doin' with that Greenhorn anyway? *[pause]* Come with me, Kate, across the river. No fences, plenty of money. You won't see a muddy hoe the rest of yer life.

KATE: Is that an intimate proposal, Frank?

FRANK: It's a straight offer.

KATE: Well you have got a nerve. First you pull up our fences then you come over talking all sweet.

FRANK: This ain't you. Look at ya.

KATE: You got no right, Frank.

FRANK: I got the right. I worked trail herds for twenty years with John Quinell. I've seen good men die on this land — for this water — an' then these nesters come an' fence it up like it was bits of cake — an' goddam it if you don't go an' join 'em. Why?

KATE: You'll have to figure that out for yerself, Frank.

[Silence.]

FRANK: Come with me.

KATE: No!

[Silence.]

FRANK: I came over to return these.

[He puts down the letters Jim wrote to Harper's Monthly.]

KATE: Jim!

[Enter Jim.]

FRANK: Mr Quinell don't appreciate the sentiments contained in these letters, Jim. All them accusations. They're an act of war.

JIM: He can't do this.

FRANK: It's his Post Office. He can do what he likes.

JIM: God damn you. Haven't you ever heard of the Constitution? You tell Quinell I want to speak with him.

FRANK: Quinell's in Washington, Mr Averill. He's talking to Congressmen about the problem we got down here with rustlers.

KATE: There ain't no more rustlers here than there ever was.

FRANK: Seems like there's been an epidemic. So the Governor is sending down a bunch of hired guns to bring these 'rustlers' to justice.

JIM: We won't leave this land, you tell that to the 'Governor'.

FRANK: This ain't a game, Jim. All the bad men this side of the Missouri are comin' this way. They'll be paid five dollars a day, an' a bonus of fifty for every rustler killed.

JIM: The government sold this land to all these homesteads along the river, and if you think we're going to let a handful of crooked, powerful men throw us off you are wrong. An' you know why, Frank? 'Cos that ain't the kind of country we want to live in.

[Frank grabs Jim.]

FRANK: You don't talk to me about this country — this country? You ain't been here an' you don't know it.

[He lets Jim go.]

FRANK: Kate, you gotta listen to me.

KATE: I listened, now get off my land.

FRANK: I warned ya — an' I'm warning you, Mister...?

CLAY: Clay.

FRANK: You ride on, 'cos you've picked one bad place to be.

[Exit Frank. Kate sits to eat.]

KATE: You ain't goin' to lose yer appetite on his account are ya, Jim?

[Jim refuses to sit.]

ANNE: Is it true what he said?

JIM: Don't you worry, we'll think of something.

ANNE: Why don't we just leave?

[Silence.]

JIM: We're not leaving.

[Jim sits to eat. They eat in silence.]

KATE: I've been thinking.

[They stop eating and regard her.]

'Bout time we had a dance up here. We'll ask all of 'em, every family along the river, the Irish, the Germans, the whole sorry bunch of 'em.

JIM: They're not Germans, they're poles 'Kopchek'.

KATE: Whatever — we'll have a real good time then we'll do some speech making, in regard to Mr Quinell's 'hired guns'. Get the folks fired up some — bunch 'em up like a fist before they start drifting away scared. We can't do nothin' on our own.

ANNE: A dance here?

KATE: Mr Kopchek senior can play the fiddle I understand.

ANNE: When?

KATE: What do you think, Jim?

JIM: What do you want my opinion for? I'm just a hired hand am I not?

[Silence. They continue to eat.]

KATE: I was thinking.

[They stop eating.]

We could get married on the same day....*[pause]* No point in feedin' the same bunch of folks twice.

JIM: Lord Jesus, you would take the wind from the sails of God's own yacht!

[Exit Jim to the fields.]

KATE: What are you starin' at?

ANNE: Nothin'.

KATE: Well go stare at it someplace else. *[exit Anne to house]* I'll guess you'll be ridin' on now, Clay. Well won't ya?

CLAY: That depends.

KATE: On what?

CLAY: If it comes to a fight here, I'd like to know what I'm defending.

[Silence.]

KATE: Some things a person got the right to put behind 'em.

[He nods and starts to rise.]

Sit down. I ran four girls from this house for six years. An' I ain't ashamed of it neither. All the cowboys came here for a good time. Even Mr Quinell. He built it for them an' paid me to run it which I did, until he begun to crave respectability and then I bought the place from him, started to run my own business. When a cowboy couldn't pay for a poke he rustled me a cow an' no one raised an eye. But then the homesteaders come an' I saw a way out, for Anne. I bought another 180 acres off the government and asked Jim down here to help me run it. I got 360 acres near enough which makes us the biggest spread this side of the river. So Quinell reckons if we go the rest will follow. *[silence]* I tried to bring Anne up the best I could. Everything I done I done for her. You make my daughter cry an' I'll make you weep.

CLAY: I ain't goin' to make her cry, Miss Watson, most likely she'll do that herself the way she throws herself at a man. Well — I'm obliged.

[Exit to fields. Anne enters and begins to clear the table. Kate strikes her across the face.]

ANNE: I hate you, an' I hate this place — an' all — an' if it burns down I won't be sorry.

[Jim and Clay are out working in the fields. Jim is pensive but Clay sings cheerfully.]

CLAY: That sweet little gal, that true little gal

That gal I left behind me
That sweet little gal that true little gal
That gal I left behind me...

JIM: What are you so cheerful about?

CLAY: Nothin'. *[silence]* Just singin' — can't a man sing out here?

JIM: Call that singing? *[Clay smiles and works]* Anne told me about those guns of yours. *[Clay stops working and stares hard at Jim]* I know she shouldn't but she did. She's wilful. *[pause]* Clay?

CLAY: What?

JIM: Quiet place like Brandonsville, guess you thought you could keep those guns wrapped up for ever. I respect that. I'm not going to ask you to use them on our behalf.

CLAY: What are you askin'?

JIM: To teach me.

CLAY: Teach you how to shoot?

JIM: What's funny about that?

[Silence.]

JIM: I have to do something.

CLAY: Then do somethin' else.

JIM: They're sending an army of cut throats down here. Am I going to stand by and let them murder us?

[Silence.]

CLAY: Puts your hands agin' mine.

[He holds his hands out in a prayer like position and Jim stands opposite in a mirror image.]

CLAY: When you feel ready, slap my jaw.

JIM: You want me to....

CLAY: Do it.

[After a few moments tension Jim tries to hit Clay but Clay wards off the blow with his left arm and strikes Jim with his right.]

JIM: What the hell are you...

CLAY: That's it, Jim, yer dead and the women are wailing. What for? So you can have some feller carve you a proud tombstone?

JIM: I'll tell you what for, Clay. Because evil is a powerful force and a man's struggle against it is bloody and everlasting.

[Silence.]

CLAY: You gotta touch of the preacher on you, Jim.

JIM: You going to help me or not?

CLAY: It's too late.

JIM: I reckon we got some weeks — maybe a month.

CLAY: I mean yer too old. You've gotta start when yer no bigger than a bar stool, when the gun's so heavy in yer hand ya near well shoot yer foot off. You gotta shoot at rocks day after day 'till yer deaf with the sound of gunfire, then you gotta progress to things that breathe an' bleed an' ya gotta kill 'em day after day till the fact of their dyin' means nothin' to ya, then you still have to face it — it ain't the same as killin' a man. *[silence]*

JIM: You misunderstand me, Clay. I'm not asking you to teach me to shoot like Wild Bill Hickock. I don't admire his kind. I'm asking you to teach me how to shoot, as straight and as true as I can.

CLAY: Straight an' true?

JIM: Well?

CLAY: Are you sayin' you can't shoot at all?

JIM: That's what I'm saying.

CLAY: You never shot a deer or a...?

JIM: No.

CLAY: Or a rabbit?

JIM: Nothing. I have a loathing of guns.

CLAY: A what?

JIM: I don't like guns.

CLAY: Why not?

JIM: Because they're the curse of this country. Isn't that why you keep those fancy pistols wrapped up in your bedroll?

CLAY: You're a remarkable man, Mr Averill. I never met your kind before.

JIM: I don't feel so remarkable, Clay. I feel small and scared. *[silence]* When I close my eyes at night I see a man walking toward me. He's dressed in black with black hair and thin black lips and he's coming down the valley with his eyes fixed on me. And I'm sweating all over because I know I'm not ready and I've got to get ready. And if it means shaking hands with the devil, I'll do it.

CLAY: I do believe you missed yer calling, Jim.

JIM: Well — I'm all out in the open — but not you. Who are you, Clay? *[silence]* I swear we could be out here fixing fences for a hundred years and I still wouldn't know you from Adam.

[Clay throws Jim his everyday Colt 44.]

CLAY: That there's a Colt 44, six shot, single action revolver, got fluted cylinders an' a spring ejection rod under the barrel — four and three quarter inches long, being what they call a civilian model. It's got an ordinary trigger guard with the spur goin' back so you wear the butt facin' back too. Weighs about two pounds. It ain't no good at distance so you get as close to yer target as ya can. For practice start at twenty paces. Hold it firmly but not stiffly, keep both eyes open an' try not to fart when yer squeezin' off.

[Silence.]

JIM: *[he smiles]* Thanks for stayin', Clay. Most men would have left by now.

CLAY: Little voice in my head told me to stay. Tells me to leave an' I'll leave.

JIM: Yeah? You could settle down here — make somethin' of yourself. Maybe with Anne.

[There is a moment's silence between the two men, then Clay starts to sing.]

CLAY: If ever I get off the trail
And the Indians they don't find me
I'll make my way straight back again
To the girl I left behind me.
[Chorus.]

[Clay begins to clap as Jim sings chorus.]

[Enter Kate into the yard.]

KATE: What in God's name is they doin' out there?

[The scene freezes and the image is held.]

ANNE: July 4th — Jim an' Ma got wed just like she said.

[The song then continues with as many verses as needed, during which the scene is created. It's the wedding day of Jim and Kate. The couple dance as if prior to the wedding as the others sing. Music.]

SONG: *['The Girl I Left Behind Me.']*

CHORUS: That sweet little gal, that true little gal
That gal I left behind me

That sweet little gal, that true little gal
That gal I left behind me.

If ever I get off the trail
And the Indians they don't find me
I'll make my way straight back again
To the girl I left behind me.

The wind did blow, the rain did flow
The hail did fall and blind me
I thought of that gal that sweet little gal
That gal I left behind me.

She wrote ahead to the place I said
I was always glad to find it
She says, 'I'm true, when you get through
Ride back and you will find me.'

When we sold out, I took the train
I knew where I would find her;
When I got back, we had a smack
And that was no gol-darned liar.

[Then the music stops. Kate sits on the porch. It's a hot, blistering day. Jim swipes away flies from a table which is covered with a white cloth and laden with food.]

KATE: Are they coming?

CLAY: No sign.

JIM: They'll come, Kate. I know these people — they'll come.

ANNE: *[to audience]* Laid out a big spread for all the folks then waited an hour or so.

JIM: Damn flies — get outta here. *[he swipes them away]* I talked to them, each one in turn — Bill Cutter shook me by the hand and said he'd be here, bring his whole family. The Kopcheks — the Dakins — all of them — they all said... God damn them — what's the matter with these people?

KATE: Maybe they don't wish to dance at no whore's wedding.

JIM: You never say that again — long as you live — long as you're my wife.

[Silence.]

ANNE: Why don't we just leave! We're not welcome here, nobody wants us, either side of the river.... *[silence]*

KATE: They must have had a meeting, or something and decided not to come otherwise a few would have made it — like you say good people.

JIM: Yeah. *[swats flies]* Where are all the good people when you need them?

CLAY: Rider comin' in.

KATE: Who is it?

CLAY: Looks like Mr Dolan.

[Jim goes inside for the rifle.]

KATE: Jim?

[Enter Frank.]

FRANK: Kate — Anne.

KATE: What do you want?

FRANK: You all have a nice wedding?

[Jim stumbles out with a rifle.]

JIM: Get off my land.

FRANK: Whoa, Jim, whoa — shoot me with that thing and there'll be nothing left but spurs.

KATE: Put it down, Jim.

FRANK: Do as your wife says, Jim — that's the first rule of marriage.

[A long pause.]

JIM: One of these days, Mr Dolan, I'll be ready for you and when I am I'll come looking. *[lowers the gun]*

FRANK: Quinell's back, he wants to talk — to the owner of this fine spread which I now understand to be you, Mr Averill.

KATE: What about?

FRANK: I don't know.

KATE: That figures, you're just a messenger aren't you, Frank? You don't pull no fences, or rough people up none, you just sit and watch and think you do nothing wrong.

FRANK: He wants to talk to Jim. Good day, Mrs Averill. Anne.

[Anne spits in his face — he grabs her but suddenly Clay has a gun at his head.]

FRANK: You're on the losing side, friend.

CLAY: Sure — that happened the day I was born.

[Exit Frank. Jim picks up his coat.]

KATE: Someone went to Quinell, told him we planned to have a meeting here today. What do you think you're doing?

JIM: I'm going to see Quinell.

KATE: Today?

JIM: Why not today. It's my wedding day — I feel cheerful.

KATE: Don't go, Jim. Please.

JIM: I have to — don't you see?

KATE: You can't — why look at you — all dressed for a wedding. And your hat all covered in flies.

[He sees Clay's hat and Clay nods and Jim takes it.]

CLAY: I'll go with ya.

JIM: This ain't your fight.

[Kate nods at Clay indicating he should go.]

ANNE: Jim?

JIM: I'll be fine — it's just talking that's all. I got a few things to say myself!

[He climbs up on the chuck wagon. The others back away and a light isolates him.]

SONG: *[Anne.]*

To the West, to the West
To the land of the free
Where the mighty Missouri
Rolls down to the sea:

[Silence.]

JIM: Whoa — Whoa —

[He pulls out the rifle.]

Who's there? Come on out.

[Enter Frank.]

FRANK: Jim.

JIM: I don't need an escort.

FRANK: I — I'm sorry about your wedding. I got nothing against you, Jim — nothing at all. *[silence]* Quinell put out the word that anyone who left their homestead for your meeting, would go back to find it burnt down. You be careful of John Quinell.

JIM: Those men you said Quinell was going to hire to take care of us 'rustlers', are they still coming?

FRANK: They're coming. Good day. *[Jim nods. Frank exits]*

JIM: *[Sings to himself.]*

Where the young may exult

And the aged may rest
Far away, far away
To the land of the West.

[A shot rings out — Jim rises startled — another shot and he collapses, dead. Music continues underneath.]

KATE: Jim — Jim *[she runs to his body and weeps over him]*

SONG: And what of the bride
Who lays down an' cries
A widow she's made
On her wedding day
Her lover he lies
'Neath the Wyoming sky
And there he may rest
In the land of the West —
Away, far away
In the land he loved best.

ANNE: We buried Jim the next day in the small cemetery which overlooks Brandonsville. People always say you get a good view of the valley from up there. The homesteaders turned out for Jim but Kate wouldn't let them near.

KATE: You get back — you hear me. You didn't come yesterday you don't come today.

[She falls by the grave.]

ANNE: If she'd have had a gun she'd 'av put a few of those long-faced folks in alongside Jim — so they backed off a distance and sung some hymns. As for Clay, he watched a while and then retrieved his hat.

[Clay takes his hat from the cross.]

END OF ACT ONE

Act Two

[Sound of a train.]

SONG: There's a bad man comin'
And he's comin' on the train
He wears a black 45
An' killin' is his fame.

He's got a fistful of notches
On the barrel of his gun
An' Wyatt Earp once swore
There was truth in every one

An' he never sleeps
Without that pistol in his paw
An' he never sits
With his back to a door

So if you see him coming
Hide yer face in fear
He's got two dark eyes
That never knowed a tear.

He had a girl who loved him
And they say he loved her back
So there's no telling why
He stepped off the track

To lead a life of death
Out in the West

Loved by nobody
Hated by the rest.

There's a bad man comin'
And he's comin' on the train
He wears a black 45
An' killin' is his fame.

[By the end of the song Cullen Masters arrives wearing black. He is met by Frank Dolan.]

MASTERS: Where's Quinell?

FRANK: Got a meetin' of the stock growers down in Cheyenne. Said fer me to meet you and give you this. *[gives him tin star]*

MASTERS: How many men we got?

FRANK: 'Bout thirty.

MASTERS: *[he checks his gun]* Best get started.

FRANK: Mr Masters? The first spread out of Brandonsville belongs to a widow named Averill. I'd like her left alone.

MASTERS: Averill?

FRANK: That's right. *[silence]*

MASTERS: You be ridin' with us, ... Mr?

FRANK: Dolan, I got things to do.

MASTERS: You and Quinell both. Best leave this business to me. Good day.

[He turns to go.]

FRANK: You can't miss the Averill place. Two storeys high, painted white. Sticks out of the prairie like old bones.

MASTERS: Mr Quinell informed me this woman Averill has eighty head of cattle — with his brand still showing.

FRANK: Take the cattle — an' the crops an' she'll leave. That's all we want.

MASTERS: Mr Quinell give me my orders, he never mentioned you, Mister... What did ya say your name was?

FRANK: Dolan.

MASTERS: I'm afraid I can't assist you in this matter.

[He turns to leave.]

FRANK: You stop there, you son of a bitch.

[Silence. Masters turns.]

MASTERS: You don't want to end up as a notch on the barrel of this gun do ya?

FRANK: Just leave her alone.

MASTERS: Still, I'm slow to anger when a man's life is involved. Life is sacred. An' I ain't in the habit of shootin' men of the law, only scum. You ain't scum are ya? Well are ya or ain't ya?

FRANK: I'll pay you. *[silence]* I said I'll pay ya.

MASTERS: You go home an' keep yer pay. Me an' the boys here will get rid of these rustlers so all you cowpokes can sleep easy. Good day to you, Mr Dolan.

[Exit Masters. Frank, visibly shaken, waits a moment.]

[Music. Kate is knocking in a fence post. She is exhausted physically and emotionally. The image should run counter to the heroic image of Clay and Jim knocking in the fence post in Act One.]

ANNE: Ma. Ma. You gotta stop. Clay, Clay, will you stop her? *[he stand impassive]* Yer hands are all bleedin'. Ma? Stop it — stop it.

[She tries to take the mallet from her mother and they

struggle till Kate falls.]

CLAY: *[softly]* Mrs Averill? Mrs Averill? *[she looks up]* Best leave the wire. It's cuttin' you to pieces. See?

[She looks at her hands. He leads her to the porch where she sits.]

CLAY: *[to Anne]* There's nothin' you can do.

[Clay goes to the lean-to.]

ANNE: Ma? Ma? Can you hear me? Would you eat something? You oughta eat.

[Kate stares out.]

This ain't no good, Ma. We've got to think what to do. We've got to find some place safe. It's not safe here. Are you listening? Ma? Ma?

KATE: Are you listening? Are Ya?

ANNE: Let go of me.

KATE: What do ya hear? — I'll tell you what I hear. I hear the Cheyenne, and the trappers, an' the buffalo and the cowboys, all of 'em who ever died in this valley, an' you know what, they're all singing. Know what they're singing?

[Anne pulls away.]

ANNE: Ma? What are you talking about?

[Silence.}

KATE: Jim was so polite.

ANNE: Jim?

KATE: He'd raise his hat to you the next day. *[pause]* You ain't ashamed of me, are ya? *[pause]* Most of 'em gold seekers never looked at ya, before, after or during. Some where closer to beasts than men, some were mean and some were cruel an' some were just cold-eyed, like Clay.

ANNE: What are you talkin' about Clay fer?

KATE: You ain't leavin' on yer own, are ya? *[silence]* He's got something bad in him.

ANNE: You don't know nothing about Clay.

KATE: That's the truth.

ANNE: Jim liked Clay. He told me. Said he was a good man.

KATE: I once saw Jim pat the head of a dog, all the time the dog was pissin' on his boots.

ANNE: You got no right to question me.

KATE: Not me? Why not me? Ain't I done enough for ya?

[Silence.]

ANNE: There's nothing here to keep me, Ma.

KATE: Nothing? You don't know what nothing is. You think Jim an' I worked our hands raw on this farm for you to call it nothing?

ANNE: I don't want it. I never wanted it.

KATE: What do you want? Shall I turn it back into a whore house an' give you a room?

[Silence.]

There's eighty head of beef, an' corn, an' alfalfa in the fields. That ain't nothin'. This town'll grow, Anne.

ANNE: It's not safe.

KATE: When the railroad touches Brandonsville, things'll change. People'll come from all over.

ANNE: We can't wait.

KATE: An' Quinell can kick an' scream but there's nothin' he'll be able to do to stop 'em comin'.

ANNE: He's hired men. Killers.

KATE: There'll be stores, different kinds sellin' different things from all over the world. An' there'll be proper sidewalks like in the East. And a jailhouse and a school and a church too, with white doors. An' folk'll nod as we walk by, and wish us good morning — just passin' the time of day, pleasantly.

[Sound of Clay's harmonica.]

KATE: Something wrong in him. I can't see what it is, but what's wrong is wrong all the way through.

ANNE: You're trying to twist me.

KATE: No I ain't.

ANNE: Ma? We have to go, can't you get that into yer head.

KATE: I'll let the grass grow over the top of this house before I let Quinell have it. That's my word.

ANNE: What about me? What about me?

KATE: What about ya? You've been fixin' to leave anyhow. Had yer eye on the skyline for the past year or so.

[She leaves her mother and turns to see Clay standing in the yard with his saddle.]

ANNE: What are you doing?

CLAY: I'm leavin'.

ANNE: You gave yer word to Jim.

CLAY: Jim's dead. *[pause]* What did you think I'd do here — shoot all the bad men for ya? *[silence]* You could come with me. Would you come with me?

ANNE: Where?

CLAY: I don't know — any place you want to go, I'll find you one just like it.

ANNE: How can I? I can't.

CLAY: I've been through a lot of towns and the graveyards is full o' folks who wouldn't leave, some shouldn't have been there in the first place. Like Jim. Like you. You don't belong here. *[silence]* You got mud on yer nose.

ANNE: She's my mother. *[silence]* What am I supposed to do?

CLAY: You stay here, you're goin' to die.

ANNE: I can't leave her — I can't.

CLAY: I once had a house an' a Ma an' Pa. Flesh an' blood. Pa traded horses down in New Mexico. One afternoon I went out shootin' ducks with my wooden gun. About sundown I heard hooves an' hid myself away. It was a war party of some kind — a whole mix of men, American, Mexican, Apache — an' they was all covered in blood like they'd just washed in it. Scalps hanging down from their saddles. Straight from Hell they looked to me, an' I knew in my bones what was goin' to happen. So I figured I could holler out an' they'd kill me but it might give my folks a chance to kill each other before them heathens reached the house. Either way I knew they was dead. I just lay still till I heard the whooping stop an' the sun had gone down an' then I left.

ANNE: Why — you tell me that?

CLAY: I did the right thing didn't I? They wanted me to live — that's what I thought. Whatever yer ma says — there's only one place she wants to be on this earth and that's inside it next to Jim Averill. That's why she's stayin' — an' she knows what's goin' to happen but she wants you to live. That's the truth. You go an' fetch what you need.

[Exit Anne. Clay approaches Kate.]

KATE: What ya doin' with my rifle?

CLAY: It was dirty. I cleaned it. *[she takes it]* I'll take good care of her. *[pause]* Why don't you come with us, Mrs Averill? You know it's wise. We can always come back when the trouble dies down. Trouble always does.

KATE: A man like Quinell don't go round the country killin' women to get what he wants. What he wants, is to be respectable.

CLAY: Your takin' a chance on that, Mrs Averill. You can't go asking Anne to take it with ya.

KATE: You'd best be runnin' then. An' if I live through this night an' find her harmed you'll have some payin' to do.

CLAY: I ain't runnin', Mrs Averill. I'm just leavin'.

[Enter Anne.]

ANNE: Come with us, Ma. Come with us, please.

KATE: Take the bay. That horse gives me nothin' but trouble anyhow.

ANNE: Ma?

KATE: Go if yer goin'.

[Exit Anne and Clay. Lights slightly fade on Kate: the setting sun.]

SONG: *[Anne.]*

Oh it's hard
On this land
To make a living I know
It raises your hopes
Then it brings 'em down low.
An' it don't give a damn
For right or for wrong
The land looks away
As we struggle along.

CHORUS: Oh the West, oh the West
Where the wild winds blow
Nobody knows, nobody knows
Nobody knows.

Now the wind
Is a howlin'
'Cross the prairie so old
It whispers an' moans
'Bout the sad buffalo.
But the land
Oh the land
Is a killer so cold
It can kill both the man
With the gun or the hoe

CHORUS: *[Repeat.]*

[During the song the actors playing Frank and Clay have become killers alongside Cullen Masters. This change to take place in view of the audience. They wear long rain coats called slickers and buttoned hats. The sun has faded and we see the scene in near darkness, the murderers almost as shadows.]

MASTERS: Mrs Averill?

KATE: Get off my land. *[she raises her rifle]*

MASTERS: You alone here?

KATE: I will be in a minute.

1st KILLER: This ain't yer land, Miss Katy, never was.

KATE: Do I know you?

1st KILLER: Sure — used to come up here regular.

2nd KILLER: How's about a farewell poke fer old time's sake?

1st KILLER: Cattle Kate. *[they laugh]*

2nd KILLER: That's a fair deal ain't it?

KATE: The deals stopped Mister, the day my husband was shot.

1st KILLER: We don't know nothin' about that.

2nd KILLER: Word is, he was out a place here anyhow.

1st KILLER: Well, Kate — how about it?

MASTERS: You heathen will be hell bound if you take one step toward that woman without my say. Mrs Averill, you have in your possession eighty head of cattle belonging to Mr John Quinell. We are here to do what the law demands concerning rustlers.

KATE: I ain't no rustler an' he knows it.

2nd KILLER: You goin' to use that piece o' iron or just wave it about some?

1st KILLER: An' hope we turn into frogs. *[they laugh]*

KATE: Get off my land. I'll count to five an' if you ain't walkin' I'll start shootin' — one — two — three — four —

1st KILLER: Whoa Jesus!

[The two killers scatter and hide but Kate's gun has jammed.]

2nd KILLER: What's the matter, Kate, didn't you clean yer piece?

1st KILLER: I always clean mine. *[they laugh]*

MASTERS: Looks like yer out of luck. *[she tries again]* Mrs Averill — put the gun down please.

[The two men emerge again and draw their guns.]

MASTERS: Put the guns away. We don't want to wake the whole valley.

[He throws a rope to one of the men who hitches it up. Kate tries to run, the other killer catches her and they fight. He laughs but is hurt. Finally he sits on her.]

1st KILLER: Ride that mare. *[he whoops and yells. Masters kicks the 2nd Killer off]*

MASTERS: Stand up, Mrs Averill, please.

[2nd Killer then pushes her over to the rope and puts it round her neck.]

MASTERS: So — this here house, was a house o' sin.

KATE: I wouldn't know. I never saw any.

MASTERS: *[angered by this, grabs her by the throat]* You're a thief. You broke the law of the nation, and the nation belongs to God, you understand me?

KATE: Don't kill me. Don't kill me. Please.

MASTERS: I can hear ya, Mrs Averill.

KATE: I'll leave. He can have it all.

MASTERS: Sing.

KATE: Sing?

MASTERS: 'My Eyes Have Seen the Glory'.

KATE: *[sings]* Of the coming of the lord
He has trampled out the vintage
Where the grapes of wrath are stored
He hath loosed his fateful lightning
With his terrible swift sword
His truth is marching on....

[They hang her. Sound of wind.]

SONG: There's been a lynching
In Johnson County
And no bounty has been claimed
Folks looked away
On that fateful day
And the killers rode off without shame.

ANNE: *[Sings.]*
Oh the West, oh the West
Where the wild winds blow
Nobody knows, nobody knows
Nobody knows.

Now the wind
Is a howlin'
Cross the prairie so old
It whispers an' moans
'Bout the sad buffalo
But the land
It don't cry
It don't shiver or sigh
It waits
And it waits
For the times to go by.

[By the end of the song the killers have gone and Frank enters, cuts the body down and hugs it. Lights fade to blackout.]

[A camp fire. Night. Clay plays the harmonica as Anne sits by the fire, distracted and tense.]

CLAY: *[stares up at the stars]* You ever get to thinking if there's life up there?

ANNE: Up where?

CLAY: On the stars. Someone up there on the Pole-star sittin' by a fire playin' a tune. I do. I get to thinkin' all kinds of things. *[pause]* Heard this feller talkin' in a bar, said the ancients knew all about the stars, how far they was away, how they got up so high in the first place. An' all this stuff the ancients knew has bin forgot, jest ground into dust over the years. Said the world was slippin' back to a time of ignorance an' hate. You think that's true?

ANNE: No.

CLAY: No?

ANNE: Things is goin' forward an' folks is getting kinder all the time. Jim said.

CLAY: I don't want to hear what Jim said. He didn't know nothing. He didn't know how to keep his hat on.

ANNE: I liked Jim an' I won't hear him spoke bad of.

[Silence.]

CLAY: Found a bone once in the desert. Guess how big that bone was?

ANNE: Can't.

CLAY: I didn't have no measure, so I laid down against it. It were one of me an a bit more.

ANNE: So?

CLAY: I stared at that bone. That bone had an effect on me.

ANNE: Why?

CLAY: Just the wonder of it.

ANNE: I don't know what yer talkin' about stars an' bones fer anyhow.

CLAY: Maybe you should get some sleep.

ANNE: Can't.

CLAY: I promised yer Ma I wouldn't let no harm come to ya — an' I won't.

ANNE: I ain't afraid. I know this country better than you.

CLAY: Guess you do.

[She buries her head in her hands.]

CLAY: *[softly]* You had no choice, Anne.

ANNE: Yes I did. Yes I did.

[She recovers her composure.]

ANNE: Ma said — told me that you was all wrong.

CLAY: *[smiles]* What she mean by sayin' that?

ANNE: I don't know.

CLAY: Maybe I am. Whole world's wrong if you ask me. We just ain't meant to be here — that's the truth as I see. If mud could speak that's what the mud would say.

ANNE: Talkin' about mud now. Stars — bones and mud!

CLAY: Just thinkin' aloud that's all. Ain't I allowed to do that? *[silence]* You got used to puttin' wire 'round things ain't ya? I can say what I want.

ANNE: I know that. You say what you want whether it's true or not.

CLAY: I always told you the truth.

ANNE: Yeah? You said yer folks was killed by an earthquake, before you had memory of them. Now you say they was murdered by savages when you was a boy. You tell me the truth or maybe I'll leave.

CLAY: Maybe I won't let you. *[she stands]* I didn't want to frighten you. Nothing wrong in that, is there?

ANNE: Tell me now.

CLAY: Tell you what?

ANNE: The truth about things.

CLAY: *[shrugs]* I don't mind — whatever.

ANNE: How'd you get that rope burn?

CLAY: Feller tried to lynch me.

ANNE: Why?

CLAY: I ain't sure. He stood me on a box — stood on that box for nearly two days. Thought I was dead.

ANNE: Why ain't ya?

CLAY: There was a miracle. Along came this funny lookin' feller called — Dickson. An' he cut me down an' I was grateful. We hitched up together for a while an' he was nice enough 'cept he had more wind in him than all the country. He sold me some lotion for the hair. I showed ya, didn't I? Said he was — I don't know — an actor. *[pause]* What else? *[silence]*

ANNE: Were you scared?

CLAY: Of what?

ANNE: Of dyin' — before this feller saved ya?

[Silence.]

CLAY: No. I ain't afraid of nothing.

[Silence.]

ANNE: Nothin' at all?

CLAY: Not anymore, not since I was a kid. My Pa used to scare me some. What else?

ANNE: I don't know. Nothin' I guess.

[Clay suddenly howls like a wolf.]

ANNE: What are you doin'?

CLAY: You want to howl, you howl. You want to dance 'round the fire, you dance. You want to cuss, go ahead an' cuss. You sure as hell can't cuss in a farmyard can ya? All the dogs a' barkin' at ya, chickens squakin'. But out here you can howl, dance an' cuss the devil who made ya, an' ee can't hear.

[He howls again.]

CLAY: Come on, come on.

[Anne howls, restrained at first, but then she lets go and they dance absurdly — howling until they collapse exhausted into each other's arms.]

CLAY: I was thinkin'.

ANNE: What?

CLAY: We should get married.

ANNE: Yeah?

CLAY: We'll find some Jesus feller in the next town. If that's what you want?

ANNE: I don't know — I guess — that would be best.

CLAY: Hell — we could have some babies?

ANNE: Do you mean it?

CLAY: Sure we could have a room full. *[she smiles]* If that's what you want.

[She kisses him, then withdraws.]

ANNE: I got to go back first, don't I?

[Silence.]

CLAY: Pa used to read me from the bible. He liked the old bits best. Said if I ever looked back I'd turn into a pillar of salt.

ANNE: I ain't never goin' to rest easy unless I do.

CLAY: An' if she's dead? If they come an' killed her?

ANNE: Then I'll bury her. *[silence]* I want us to be happy, Clay. We won't be, unless I go back.

[Clay paces up and down in an agitated, dangerous

way.]

You won't try to stop me, will ya?

CLAY: No — I won't stop ya. I was just foolin'. *[she kisses him]*

[Music. Frank is finishing the burial of Kate. He knocks in a cross with the flat of his spade. Then he takes off his hat. His figure is silhouetted against a blood-red sky.]

ANNE: *[off]* Ma — Ma.

[Frank hears the voice and hides. Enter Clay and Anne.]

CLAY: She ain't here I tell ya.

ANNE: Ma.

CLAY: Maybe she's gone someplace safe.

ANNE: There's been horses here. Ma! *[exit]*

CLAY: *[calls after her]* She ain't here. *[Frank enters, his gun pointed at Clay's head]*

FRANK: Put yer hands behind yer head. Get on your knees.

ANNE: *[off faintly]* Ma?

CLAY: Where is she Frank?

FRANK: She's dead. Lynched.

CLAY: What are you doin' here?

FRANK: Shut up.

[Enter Anne.]

ANNE: What — are you doin'? Where's my Ma?

CLAY: Tell her.

ANNE: Where is she?

CLAY: Tell her, Frank.

FRANK: They killed her. Man called Masters come an' killed her. Did it for Quinell — I warned her didn't

I?

[Anne sits in a crumpled heap.]

FRANK: I — I didn't know you was comin' back. So I buried her up there — next to Jim.

CLAY: Guess you was just passin' by.

FRANK: I had nothing to do with it, Anne. I swear.

CLAY: But you knew — why didn't you stop him? Did you try?

FRANK: You keep talkin' an' I'll blow yer head off.

CLAY: Did you get scared? Did he scare you some?

[After a moment's tension Frank lowers the gun.]

FRANK: I did what I could.

[Anne picks up her mother's rifle. Frank puts his hand on it. They stand.]

ANNE: Let go of me.

[He lets go of the rifle.]

Go away, Frank. Just go away.

FRANK: The governor's down in Cheyenne. When he hears what Masters done in his name he'll pull them killers out. That'll be the end of it.

[Exit Frank. Anne sits again and rocks to and fro.]

ANNE: Clay?

CLAY: *[softly]* I'm here.

ANNE: Hold me. *[he does so]* What am I goin' to do?

CLAY: We'll just sit here an' rest awhile.

ANNE: I'm so confused, Clay.

CLAY: Sssh now.

ANNE: I hate this house. I hate this whole country. It's

mean an' it's cruel an' it's bad.

CLAY: It's not all bad. We found a little good together ain't we? Well?

ANNE: I'm so tired. So tired.

[She rests her head on his shoulder.]

CLAY: Sssh now. *[lights fade]*

[The saloon is represented by a saloon singer — and two poker tables, one chair at each. At one table sits Cullen Masters playing solitaire. As this scene is being created the saloon singer sings the following song.]

SONG: Come listen to this tragedy
It'll make yer blood run cold
The story of a gunfight
So foolish, yet so old.

Whatever was their argument
I never heard of yet
Perhaps it was about a girl
More likely just a bet.

Now the street is all deserted
The window blinds are down
The sun has risen someplace high
Above this Western town.

The wind it hardly dares to breathe
An' time stands still with fear
As death is walkin' down the street
His spurs you softly hear. *[musical change]*

A flash of light
A burst of sound
One man stands
The other falls
Gently to the ground.

He gives a little frightened sigh
As he sees the clouds go racin' by

An' all his pride an' all his pain
Goes ridin' over, to the other side.

The story of a gunfight
Is the story of our day
The man who dies for nothin'
And the man who walks away....

[Clay enters as the song finishes in the suit of buckskin, the white hat, the two guns with pearl handles and a pair of spurs. The music stops as he enters and Cullen Masters and the singer both regard him with worldly amusement. The music may begin again as Clay approaches the table opposite Masters.]

SINGER: That's a mighty fine outfit you got there, son.

CLAY: Yeah, ain't it?

SINGER: You look real dandy.

CLAY: Thanks.

SINGER: You want one of the girls to keep you company?

CLAY: No. Just a drink.

SINGER: Get it yerself. I ain't a waitress. *[the singer moves away]*

CLAY: Can I buy you a drink, sir, seeing as yer all alone?

MASTERS: No thank you.

CLAY: Well — this is a hogranch ain't it? *[silence]* A rattlesnake would be ashamed to meet his mother in here — oops, don't tell me, yer mother works upstairs. *[he laughs in a friendly way]* Well — how long you bin in here sir, paintin' yer nose all red?

MASTERS: Do I know you?

CLAY: Yes, sir.

MASTERS: Remind me. *[Clay mimes being hung]* Clay.

CLAY: Seems like you held another hemp party, but I

weren't invited this time.

MASTERS: What do you want?

CLAY: I come to take you home.

MASTERS: Chew that finer for me.

CLAY: You hung me up to die an' I died. Then these angels in buckskin come around an' give me this hat an' these good lookin' guns an' then they said I had to come back an' fetch the man what killed me.

MASTERS: *[smiles]* Guess you're some kind of ghost then?

CLAY: No, I'm an angel.

MASTERS: Is that right?

CLAY: That's right.

MASTERS: Never figured on you gettin' to heaven, Clay. What you see up there?

CLAY: Nothin' — no whores — no saloons, no whiskey neither. Guess even a God fearin' man like you gotta have one weakness.

MASTERS: This ain't whiskey, son. This is soda pop.

CLAY: Soda pop? No. You mean I'm goin' to be known as the man who shot the soda pop kid? Hell, that ain't fair. *[silence]*

MASTERS: Clay — I confess you worry me some. Under my employ you shot at least six men — all through the back, not to mention their women and their children. Now you come on all courageous.

CLAY: That's easy, Mr Masters. I'm tryin' to impress a young lady.

MASTERS: Yeah? Does she know yer an angel?

CLAY: Sure. She really does. She really does.

[Silence.]

MASTERS: You fuckin' crazy son of a bitch.

[As he says this they draw and shoot in slow motion. For a moment we don't know which man has been shot. Then Cullen Masters falls dead. A moment's silence. Then the saloon singer begins to sing.]

SINGER: A flash of light
A burst of sound
One man stands
The other falls
Gently to the ground.
He gives a little frightened sigh
As he sees the clouds
Go racin' by
An' all his pride
An' all his pain
Goes ridin' over
To the other side.

The story of a gunfight
Is the story of our day
The man who died for nothin'
And the man who walks away.

[Clay is sitting on the porch of the house or by the table outside. He reads to Anne. It is morning.]

CLAY: "Pictured above is an artist's impression of the man who shot and killed the notorious gunman Cullen Masters in a bar in Brandonsville, Johnson County, Wyoming. The man who has not been identified entered the premises known locally as 'The Bucket of Blood' at approximately twelve noon on August 10th. He was wearing a suit of pale buckskin, a white hat and brandished two finely made Colt 45 Peacemakers with pearl handles. Witnesses say that this outfit was at first the subject of some amusement but the bar room swiftly emptied when the stranger made his intentions clear. Within five minutes of noon Mr Masters lay dead on the floor. His assailant vanished as mysteriously as he had come. It's believed that he is being protected by local homesteaders whose cause he was defending at the time of the incident."

ANNE: Thought you couldn't read.

CLAY: Get some coffee. *[she turns to go but then turns back]*

ANNE: Clay? Clay?

CLAY: Stop sayin' my name like that. Clay, Clay, like some little dog yappin'. *[pause]* What they give this feller a moustache fer? He don't look like me at all.

ANNE: You ought to take that suit an' burn it. Then we could stay here.

CLAY: What you want to stay for?

[Silence.]

When yer Ma was alive you was itchin' to leave, now she's dead you want to stay. Is that what you wanted, to have the place to yerself?

ANNE: Why d'ya say that? You know it ain't true.

CLAY: Maybe I'll sell the place.

ANNE: How can you sell it? It ain't yours.

CLAY: I fought for it, didn't I? *[pause]* Ain't nothin' but an old whore house anyhow. What are you lookin' at?

ANNE: Nothin'.

CLAY: Maybe we oughta burn it to the ground.

ANNE: Why?

CLAY: 'Cos it's made o' wood.

[Silence.]

ANNE: Anyway I — I don't feel up to travellin' just now.

CLAY: Why not? What are ya saying?

ANNE: I'm goin' to have a baby.

[Silence.]

CLAY: That's real nice.

ANNE: Aren't you glad? You said you would be.

CLAY: Sure I'm glad. *[he sits and takes out his guns]*

ANNE: What are you doin'?

CLAY: I'm cleanin' my gun — what's it look like I'm doin'?

ANNE: Clay?

CLAY: Will you stop saying that.

ANNE: There's a rider crossed the ford.

CLAY: *[doesn't look up]* Who?

ANNE: It's Frank Dolan.

CLAY: Best get some coffee — like I said.

ANNE: Coffee?

CLAY: We ain't turned a soul from the door yet and we ain't goin' to start today. *[Anne stares at him momentarily then exits. Enter Frank]*

CLAY: Mornin' Frank — *[silence]* Wanna buy some cattle — all neatly branded with the big Q? *[he laughs]*

FRANK: Where's Anne?

CLAY: She's fixin' some coffee for ya. *[pause]* Well — the governor pulled out those bad men just like you said, Frank. I knew we could trust you. *[pause]* How is the new job?

FRANK: Interesting.

CLAY: Sure as hell beats pullin' stupid cows from bog holes don't it? I heard some fellers in Fort Worth a while back an' they was weeping in their beers 'no more trails'. Hell — I rode trail, Frank, a thousand miles an' I ate as much dust as a man can. I reckon the sun done gone addled their brains.

[Anne enters holding a jug of coffee but she stands, uncertain whether or not to approach as if under Clay's influence she's losing any will of her own.]

CLAY: Tell Frank the glad news, Anne. *[silence]* We's going to be proud parents. I am so thrilled. I can't tell ya. *[silence]* Pour the man a coffee. *[she does so and Clay continues cleaning his gun]* What's on yer mind, Sheriff?

FRANK: *[pause]* Nothin'.

CLAY: Nothing? Come a long way to say that. *[pause]* Don't stand there sweatin', Frank, say what you came for.

[Silence.]

CLAY: You ain't come to arrest me have ya?

FRANK: No.

CLAY: Just being friendly?

FRANK: That's it.

CLAY: It was self-defence anyhow — you know that don't ya? Masters drew first, give me no choice.

FRANK: That's as I heard.

CLAY: I don't know why you was so jittery about him, Frank. He was mortal as can be. More blood in him than an ox. Still, that's all in the past, ain't it? *[Frank nods]* You should drink that — put some colour back in ya.

FRANK: Maybe I will.

CLAY: She ain't feelin' social on a cause of her condition. You understand.

[Frank drinks. As he raises the cup to his lips Clay hits him viciously over the side of the head with the barrel of his gun. Frank falls and Clay stands over him pointing the gun at his head.]

ANNE: Clay? Clay — don't.

CLAY: Why'd you come here, Frank? What d'ya want?

FRANK: Nothin'.

[Clay hits him again.]

ANNE: Clay!

CLAY: You dragged up men from Hell to kill these folks an' now you walk around wearin' that dumb badge like nothin' happened. *[he hits him again]* You come here to take me in? Yeah? An when the time come yer nerve broke didn't it, Frank, same as it did when you squared up against Masters. Maybe you ain't cut out to be a lawman, Frank — maybe yer just an' old cowpoke whose day is done.

[He drags Frank's body to a post and ties him to it.]

ANNE: Clay. *[he turns and hits her. The blow takes her so much by surprise she hardly reacts at all — but falls and stands up again]*

CLAY: I gotta think what to do here.

ANNE: Where are you goin'?

CLAY: I got to think what's best for you and me and Frank. I got to figure some things out, alone, you understand that, don't ya?

[He touches her cheek tenderly.]

ANNE: Sure, sure.

CLAY: I won't be long — just need some time. *[exit Clay]*

FRANK: Anne? Anne — you hearin' me? *[she looks at him]* You get away from him now — you run.

ANNE: Best be quiet, Frank, or I'll burn this house down on yer head. I truly will.

[Silence.]

FRANK: I kept thinkin' when I found yer Ma — why didn't she let off a few shots — I checked the gun. It was jammed full o' dirt. Who'd do that?

ANNE: I said be quiet.

FRANK: Then Jim. Where was Clay when Jim died? Where was he, Anne?

ANNE: Here!

FRANK: Here?

ANNE: *[she thinks]* Ma asked him to keep watch over Jim, save him from gettin' bushwhacked.

FRANK: He did it, Anne. He's one mad dog.

ANNE: You don't talk about him like that — you hear.

FRANK: Couple of mountain men come down yesterday, said they'd found the remains of a man up in the hills. Found a picture in his coat — a man wearing a buckskin suit an' a white hat an' holdin' a couple of fancy pistols. Man's name was Dickson — Elias Dickson. He'd been shot in the back.

ANNE: There ain't no picture.

FRANK: It's right here in my coat — get it.

ANNE: He should have killed you.

FRANK: He probably will. An' he'll kill you as well without battin' an eye. Ain't that why he's gone out there? To settle his mind on it. Anne?

ANNE: Why'd you come back here, Frank?

FRANK: I owed you. Picture's right here — Anne — please. *[she takes it out and looks at it without expression]* He's no good.

ANNE: He's as good as you.

[They sit waiting. Time passes, as if the day continues until sunset. Enter Clay.]

CLAY: Wake up, Frank. *[kicks him]*

ANNE: Clay?

CLAY: I've been through it all ways. I know you'd like to stay here, be near yer Ma and Jim an' all — but I can't. I ain't a farmer. Simple as that.

ANNE: *[nods]* What about the house?

CLAY: Leave it. It's just a thing — it ain't important. *[pause]* We won't travel fast, keep an easy pace so it don't upset ya.

ANNE: Where are we going?

CLAY: Someplace good for a child, where they got doctors an' schoolin'. Them things is goin' to be important. Old ways is over, ain't that right, Frank? *[to Anne]* We's going to be sad if we do aught else. *[softly]* You go fetch the things ya need.

[Exit Anne.]

CLAY: You still sweatin', Frank?

FRANK: You goin' to kill me? In front of her?

CLAY: Maybe. She'd understand.

FRANK: Well do it then.

CLAY: Don't be brave, Frank — it don't become ya. *[shows him the paper]* You seen this?

FRANK: No.

CLAY: Picture of me lookin' Dandy.

FRANK: Yer folks'll be proud of ya.

CLAY: Oh. I ain't got folks no more, they was killed.

FRANK: Yeah? How come?

CLAY: *[gently]* I shot 'em.

FRANK: Jim too?

CLAY: Yes, sir.

FRANK: Why?

CLAY: Had the chance. I don't want you to worry for me, Frank.

FRANK: I ain't worried for you.

CLAY: *[smiles]* It don't matter, Frank. What you or me, say or do, 'cos it'll all be lost on the wind by tomorrow. That's the truth, Frank — nothing matters 'cos we're all just passin' through — an' none of us is happy in our skins. And the moment you know that — there's nothing to be or belong to you can be free. Hell, it's a free country.

[Enter Anne with suitcase.]

ANNE: I'm ready.

[As Clay reaches for the case with one hand Anne steps forward and stabs him with a knife. He moves away then falls. Anne moves to him and kneels and strokes his hair.]

ANNE: What do you see?

CLAY: Nothin'. *[he smiles]* Nothin' at all — don't you worry none —

[He dies.]

SONG: *[Single voice.]*

To the West
To the West
To the land of the free
Where the mighty Missouri
Rolls down to the sea
Where the young may exalt
And the aged may rest

Away far away
In the land of the West.

[By the time the song has finished the image of Clay's death has faded. Anne sits down on the porch as at the beginning of Act One. Young Dickson enters.]

STORY-TELLERS: It was a Sunday
In the late Fall of 1935
Johnson County Wyoming.

Miss Anne Watson, sixty years of age,
Sat on the porch of her house
Watching the sun sink slowly in the west.

ANNE: A few months after, I got some post. I don't know who sent it. Frank, maybe. Inside the envelope was an old wanted poster. All yella — an' faded. It showed a boy aged seventeen or so wanted for the murder of his Ma an' Pa in Texas. He'd shot 'em as they lay sleepin'. Boy's name was Charles Lee Arthur Yates.

DICKSON: Clay?

ANNE: Boy was never found but I guess it was him. *[pause]* It was him. *[pause]* Sometimes he comes to me in dreams, an' I want him to. Don't ask me to figure it, 'cos I hate him, I hate him truly. *[silence]* I dream a lot these days, Mr Dickson. Mind wanders off. I see Ma an' Jim sitting out here on the porch talkin' about what this country is goin' to be. *[she smiles. silence]* Well — any more questions for me, Mr Dickson?

DICKSON: Uh — well I — what happened to John Quinell?

ANNE: The homesteads were too small. Folks done badly an' borrowed money. When they couldn't repay Quinell bought them out and they became tenants. Bin tenants ever since.

DICKSON: You've been Quinell's tenant?

ANNE: An' his son after. What's the matter, Mr Dickson?

DICKSON: It seems so unfair, so wrong.

ANNE: *[shrugs]* I never met Quinell, not once, but I saw his pitcher one time in the paper. I swear the way he was grinnin' it was Uncle Sam his self. *[she sighs]* I'm gettin' tired, Mr Dickson.

DICKSON: Just one more thing — Ma'am — would you happen to know if my Grandfather ever — if he was ever brought down and given a Christian burial?

ANNE: No. He's out there somewhere. Ain't that good enough for Ya?

[Pause.]

DICKSON: Maybe it's better.

ANNE: Wait here. *[she goes in and comes back with the guns and the white hat and the carpet bag]* Best take 'em.

DICKSON: May I? *[she shrugs]* Do you have the photo...

ANNE: It's in the bag.

[He takes it out.]

DICKSON: Thank you. Thank you. You don't know how much this means to me.

ANNE: Looks a darned fool, don't 'ee?

DICKSON: Oh — I don't know. Well — it's gettin' late. I best be on my way. *[he fetches his bicycle]* Miss Watson?

ANNE: Ask it?

DICKSON: What happened to your child?

ANNE: Grew up an left. Went East.

DICKSON: I see. Well I — thanks so much.

[He has some difficulty in holding the bike and putting the bag on. Anne watches him struggling. He has

nowhere to put the hat.]

Guess I'll just have to wear it back to Brandonsville.

ANNE: Guess you will.

DICKSON: Goodbye, Miss Watson — thank you. *[cycles away]*

SONG: *[Led by Anne.]*

Oh it's hard
On this land
To make a living I know
It raises your hopes
Then it brings 'em down low
'An it don't give a damn
For right or for wrong
The land looks away
As we struggle along

Oh the West
Oh the West
Where the wild wind blows
Nobody knows nobody knows
Nobody knows

Now the wind
Is a howlin'
Cross the prairie so old
It whispers an' moans
'Bout the sad buffalo
But the land
It don't cry
It don't shiver or sigh
It waits
And it waits
For the times to go by.

CHORUS: *[Anne's voice.]*

Oh the West, oh the West
Where the wild winds blow

Nobody knows, nobody knows
Nobody knows.

THE END

Paradise Drive

Notes to the Original Production

First performance: Albert Road Community Centre, Penarth on Wednesday, 22nd February, 1989.

Cast

Jennifer.................................Gaynor Lougher
Sally...Eddie Ladd
John.......................................Matthew Bailey
David..Richard Berry

Director................................Rosamunde Hutt
Music Director........................Philip Thomas
Designer................................Richard Aylwin
Stage Manager.......................Gillian Dearne

Act One

SCENE ONE

DAVID: *[As narrator.]*

May 2nd, 1979. The eve of the General Election. A House in the suburbs of a city. Enter Jennifer, a woman in her late thirties. She carries two table cloths. In a mesmeric fashion she spreads them, one after the other, on the family table. *[one of them is Indian, reminiscent of the 1960's]* Sally, her daughter, aged 16, arrives home from school. She watches her mother for a moment.

JENNIFER: Sally!

SALLY: What are you doing? It's six o'clock!

JENNIFER: I thought it was a nice idea, but I couldn't bring myself to put it on.

SALLY: Do it, do it! *[she helps her mother spread the Indian cloth]*

JENNIFER: It's still beautiful, isn't it?

SALLY: Mum, they'll be home soon. We can't be late, not tonight.

JENNIFER: John's home, he's upstairs reading.

SALLY: He said he couldn't be here till 6:30. Is the food in? *[she dumps her school bags and begins laying the table]*

JENNIFER: I've done the place names.

SALLY: What about the food?

JENNIFER: It's in the oven, it will only take half an hour.

SALLY: What is it?

JENNIFER: I hope David won't be late — he said something about a working lunch.

SALLY: Mum —

[Jennifer stops, looks at Sally, worried.]

What is it?

JENNIFER: What?

SALLY: In the oven. What are we having?

JENNIFER: Fish pie.

SALLY: And?

JENNIFER: I thought we'd have a salad.

SALLY: Is it done?

JENNIFER: It's in the oven.

SALLY: The salad! Is the salad done?

JENNIFER: It's all there, Sally, waiting.

SALLY: I'll do it.

JENNIFER: I've done the place names. Two of them.

SALLY: These are new. *[she picks up a knife]*

JENNIFER: I bought them for the occasion.

SALLY: Mum.

JENNIFER: I couldn't resist. They looked so inviting, beautiful.

SALLY: Where's the cake?

JENNIFER: It's not time for the cake.

SALLY: I know it's not time for the cake, but you asked me to buy candles and they need to be put on the cake.

JENNIFER: I'll get changed then.

SALLY: Where's the cake?

JENNIFER: In the cake tin.

[Exit Sally. While she is out Jennifer takes off the cutlery that has been laid and removes the Indian table cloth and replaces it with the grey one. Sally enters with the cake.]

SALLY: Mum?

JENNIFER: I don't know.

SALLY: I thought you were going to get changed.

JENNIFER: When I've finished the place names. For John I put "John, eighteen today". And for Dad "Life begins at forty". I couldn't think of anything else. I sat in the potting shed for hours and thought and thought but I couldn't get an idea.

[Pause.]

SALLY: Mum. It's alright. It's alright.

[Enter John. Sally covers the cake.]

JOHN: I didn't get Dad a card. We did agree didn't we?

SALLY: Agree what?

JOHN: Not to get him a card. He said he didn't want us to waste money on cards.

SALLY: I'd already made him one.

JOHN: But he said he didn't want cards.

JENNIFER: I don't think he meant that he didn't want cards.

JOHN: I didn't get him a card because he said he despised the trite messages.

JENNIFER: That's what he said... he didn't mean....

JOHN: And now you've got him one and it will look like I didn't get him one.

SALLY: Which you didn't. *[pause]* Go and buy a stupid card. You're not meant to be here till 6:30 anyway.

Go on, go, go, go, go, go. *[they tussle]*

JENNIFER: And buy some matches. *[they stop and look at her]* For the fire.

SALLY: Well go on.

[Exit John.]

[to Jennifer] We haven't got a fire.

JENNIFER: I didn't want to say cake. *[they work]* School alright? Violin practice.

SALLY: Yes — if I have to.

JENNIFER: You promised. *[pause]* It's been an odd day. Nothing on the radio except politicians and opinion polls, no stories. *[pause]* Did you know John could read in French?

SALLY: What?

JENNIFER: I went up to tidy his room. *[Sally throws her a look]* Just to tidy up and I found this book in French and I never knew. He was no good at French in school — no good at anything except drawing, now he's reading in French and not saying anything. Why didn't he say he was interested in French?

SALLY: He doesn't have to 'say' everything.

JENNIFER: Well we can't help him now. He's going. It's too late. He should have said.

SALLY: I wouldn't worry. He'll be home every Sunday. For something to eat.

JENNIFER: David and I went to France once. Paris. It was lovely.

SALLY: When was that?

JENNIFER: *[thinks]* The year before '68.

SALLY: '67.

JENNIFER: The year before '68. There were riots in Paris in '68.

That's how I remember.

SALLY: What kind of riots?

JENNIFER: Student riots... an uprising, more than a riot.

SALLY: Were you there?

JENNIFER: No, we were there in '67.

SALLY: That was the year before '68, I'm sure of it.

JENNIFER: I wish John had said he was interested in French.

[Jennifer begins to re-lay the table and put on the Indian cloth.]

SALLY: What are you doing now?

JENNIFER: It won't take a minute.

SALLY: We're going to be late, and I can't be late, not tonight.

JENNIFER: Then help me. *[Sally decides not to lose her temper and helps her mother]*

SALLY: Are you sure you want this on?

JENNIFER: It's for David.

SALLY: It's John's birthday too.

[Jennifer takes this in and begins to remove the Indian table cloth.]

SALLY: No, no, put it back. Sorry, sorry, sorry, sorry, sorry.

[Enter John. Sally hides the cake.]

SALLY: That was quick.

JOHN: I changed my mind.

JENNIFER: No matches then?

SALLY: I've got matches, don't worry about matches.

JENNIFER: Why have you got matches?

[John sits at the table.]

SALLY: You can't sit there, heart-throb, we're busy.

JENNIFER: Go and have a bath, John.

JOHN: I had a bath this morning.

SALLY: It's your birthday, have another bath.

[John opens his book.]

SALLY: For God's sake, John. You'll spoil everything.

JENNIFER: No, no.

[They look at Jennifer and decide not to argue. John leaves.]

You're not smoking are you?

SALLY: Sometimes. Not very often.

JENNIFER: I'll get changed then. *[exit]*

[Sally goes to John's room.]

SALLY: Listen, listen, listen, listen.

[Silence.]

JOHN: What?

SALLY: I can't stay long tonight, and we're late. But I'll stay for the meal. If I can. *[John nods]* I'm going out with Trevor. You remember Trevor? *[John nods]* I'll stay for the meal, okay?

JOHN: That's fine.

SALLY: Jane Phillips was asking after you. She said she's not interested in schoolboys any more. Wants someone with a proper job, money, money.

JOHN: Warehouse packing isn't a proper job.

SALLY: You get paid don't you?

JOHN: If that's what counts, then it's a proper job.

SALLY: You're so bloody snotty. It's only a summer job for you. *[silence]* What shall I tell Jane then?

JOHN: Nothing.

SALLY: Don't you want a girlfriend?

JOHN: I don't 'want' anyone.

SALLY: What do you 'want' then? Come on. I won't tell anyone. I'm serious. What do you really want, John?

[John challenges her with his gaze.]

JOHN: Love beyond life.

SALLY: What?

JOHN: Now go away.

SALLY: I didn't hear what you said.

JOHN: Yes you did.

SALLY: I didn't — say it again.

JOHN: No.

SALLY: I want to know what you said. I didn't hear.

JOHN: Go away.

SALLY: You said something and I'm not leaving this room until you say it again — if you said it once you can say it twice — go on — I'm not leaving until...

JOHN: I said — love beyond life.

[Silence.]

SALLY: 'LOVE BEYOND LIFE' *[she considers this]* I don't think that's what Jane Phillips had in mind. What she had in mind was a bit more — 'sticky'.

JOHN: Go away.

[David, their father, enters. He wears his working clothes, a suit that today is a little dishevelled. David works for British Rail in publicity and marketing. It is his 40th birthday. Sally leaves John and crosses to him.]

DAVID: Sally. *[she is instantly aware that he is slightly intoxicated]* You've got paper clips in your thingummy.

SALLY: Yes, Dad — I know.

DAVID: Ah. Point taken.

[Sally exits.]

Sally! Sally!

[Enter Jennifer, dressed for the occasion.]

DAVID: Sorry I'm late.

JENNIFER: I put your suit out.

DAVID: What for?

JENNIFER: Your suit — it's on the bed.

DAVID: I don't want to change into another suit. I want to relax. There's no one else coming is there?

JENNIFER: No, just us.

DAVID: No need for another suit then.

JENNIFER: No. I'll put it back.

DAVID: What's this?

[Thinking that David has noticed the table cloth, Jennifer turns, but he has picked up a piece of the new cutlery.]

JENNIFER: I bought them for the occasion.

DAVID: We have two sets of cutlery, unused, in the sideboard. Why?... *[he sighs and puts it down]* Well, they're very attractive. *[pause]* All three sets are very attractive. *[she stares at him and he catches her meaning instantly]* They took me out for a lunchtime drink, that's all. To celebrate.

JENNIFER: The office?

DAVID: A few of them. Richard, Anna Marie. Richard said

the Family Railcard promotion was "first class" and wished me Happy Birthday with a significant nod of his head. *[David demonstrates]* You know. *[Jennifer looks blank]* It's code. More money, I think. You get to recognise the winks and nods, if you're lucky. *[he now notices the table cloth]* What's this?

JENNIFER: I found it upstairs in the trunk. *[pause]* You remember.

DAVID: What? Remember what? *[Jennifer exits]* Jennifer?

[John enters.]

Have you ever seen this table cloth before?

JOHN: No. Dad — I didn't get you a birthday card because you said you didn't want one, and I took you at your word.

DAVID: Thank you. *[John goes back to his room leaving David bemused]* John? Very thoughtful.

[David pours himself a drink and drinks steadily through the rest of the scene. He picks up a bread roll and absent-mindedly begins to eat it, then, realising he shouldn't do this, puts it back. He approaches John's room.]

DAVID: How was work?

JOHN: The same.

DAVID: You'll be at college soon. *[pause]* Thought about tomorrow?

JOHN: Yes.

DAVID: Any advice?

JOHN: *[pause]* Do you mean you're not going to vote Labour?

DAVID: How about you?

JOHN: But you've always said....

DAVID: Not everything's written in stone, John. Besides, it's your vote, not mine. Well. I'll leave you to your book. Thanks.

[Jennifer enters.]

JENNIFER: Right, we're all set. David — John — Sally.

DAVID: John, Sally, come on.

[They converge on the table.]

DAVID: Very attractive.

JENNIFER: You've got paper clips. There.

DAVID: Ssssshh. Don't you recognise a political statement when you see one?

SALLY: It's not a political statement.

DAVID: I was joking. A joke.

SALLY: Happy Birthday. *[she thrusts a card at him]*

JENNIFER: Next to your Dad.

SALLY: And one for you, lover-boy.

JOHN: Thanks.

DAVID: What a disgusting card!

[Sally is delighted.]

SALLY: Made it myself.

DAVID: Even worse than last year. Congratulations.

[Sally and David laugh together at this. Jennifer and John smile but are not part of it.]

JENNIFER: You wouldn't believe the time she spent on them. I mean the time you invested.

DAVID: We know what you mean.

JOHN: Thanks, Sally. No, really. It's great.

SALLY: Well I'm not 'the artist'.

DAVID: Oh, I don't know. Anything passes for Art these days. Now I've a little something for you. *[he gives an envelope to John and they fall silent as he opens it]*

JOHN: Money... It's money.

DAVID: Help you through the first year.

JOHN: Thanks very much — really.

DAVID: Artists have to eat, even abstract ones. Ha!

JENNIFER: For you, and for you. *[she gives each a small box]* It's just a keepsake for the occasion.

DAVID: Ah! *[he looks at the present quizzically]*

SALLY: It's a shell Dodo!

JENNIFER: Sally!

DAVID: I can see it's a shell.

JENNIFER: It's difficult to find ones which are unspoilt these days. I searched for hours.

JOHN: It's beautiful.

DAVID: Yes, it's a very attractive shell, and the box too.

SALLY: She painted it herself.

DAVID: Yes, I can see that, Sally — it's hand painted — you see, John?

JOHN: *[to Jennifer]* Thank you. For both.

DAVID: Shell and box. Very attractive. Indeed.

JENNIFER: Here's to David and John

[They raise glasses.]

DAVID: Success, happiness, etcetera.

[They drink and Sally and Jennifer get up.]

DAVID: That's it is it? The cutlery was just a diversion?

JOHN: *[mouths]* 'The Cake' *[exit Jennifer and Sally]*

DAVID: Ah. Now? *[silence]* I passed by your new flat this afternoon. I looked in the window.

JOHN: Why?

DAVID: There's quite a lot of work to do, isn't there? Before you can move in. Decorating. Your Mum's very good at decorating. Painting. But I don't think she'll ask.

JOHN: I'd like to do it myself. I don't want to hurt her. I just want to decorate it myself.

[Silence.]

DAVID: She's always been good at painting. That's where you get it from. *[pause]* Very attractive shells, aren't they? *[pause]* She made a necklace once out of shells, years ago, she wore them to pop concerts. So many people admired them I thought we should go into business. *[pause]* Have you ever seen this table cloth before?

JOHN: Are you drunk?

DAVID: *[shakes his head]* It was Anna Marie. Kept filling my glass at lunch. What are they doing?

[Violin plays. Enter Sally playing the violin and Jennifer carrying the cake with candles. They sing 'Happy Birthday'. Jennifer puts the cake down.]

ALL:
SONG: *['Tenderness']*

Every meal of our lives,
In the house and in the heart,
Every meal of our lives,
A quartet make their communion,
Living only in the warmth,
The warmth of warm ones around us.
Every day and every meal of our lives.
In the house and in the heart,
Every communion is a giving
And a receiving.

The taste of the food on the table,
And the light, the light in the room,
And the peace,
The peace and wholeness of the moment,
In the house and in the heart,
And in the love
The taste of the food upon the table,
And the tenderness,
The tenderness.

[They blow the candles out.]

DAVID: When I think of the sounds that used to come out of that violin.

JOHN: Thanks, Sal.

DAVID: And the cake! *[he pours drink]*

JENNIFER: The food will only be a minute.

[David looks at the table cloth. Sally looks at her watch.]

JENNIFER: I was thinking, John, about the flat. If it's too expensive —

JOHN: What?

JENNIFER: David and I were talking about the loft just the other day. We could convert it into an artist's studio, you could still live here and work up there. You'd hardly have to come downstairs at all. *[silence]* It does seem a pity to spend all that money on rent — you could spend it on paint, brushes, canvas. *[silence]* It could be ready by September.

DAVID: I do recognise this cloth. Didn't we once... *[he thinks]* Good God!

SALLY: He's drunk.

DAVID: I certainly am not.

JOHN: What about the cloth?

DAVID: Wouldn't you like to know.

JOHN: Know what?

JENNIFER: David.

JOHN: Know what?

SALLY: Leave him alone, he's drunk.

DAVID: I am not drunk.

JOHN: What about the cloth?

DAVID: What about it? You were conceived under this cloth. Or at least thought about. *[silence. Jennifer bows her head]* Why on earth have you got it on the table?

SALLY: I've got to go.

DAVID: Go?

SALLY: I promised Tevor, and everything's so late.

DAVID: Sit down, Sally.

JOHN: I don't mind. I really don't mind.

SALLY: Please, Dad, he'll be waiting.

DAVID: Sit down.

JOHN: I don't mind.

DAVID: What about the meal? Your mother's cooked a meal. It's an occasion.

JOHN: Won't anyone listen? I said, I don't mind.

JENNIFER: It's David's birthday too!

[Freeze.]

END OF ACT ONE

Act Two

SALLY: *[As narrator.]*

August, 1981. Two years have passed. John is now at Art School and happy there. He is home for the holidays. Jennifer has sought new interests, while David has worked hard and gained promotion at British Rail.

[Jennifer is practising her Yoga. David enters. It is late. He looks at the suitcase which lies on the table and dreams of deserted beaches.]

DAVID: When did she phone?

JOHN: I told you, last night.

DAVID: Why did she call you and not us?

JOHN: I don't know.

DAVID: Museums, you said?

JOHN: She said.

DAVID: Has she got a boyfriend in London? *[pause]* It wouldn't matter. I mean, she's eighteen, we'd understand, but it would be nice to know where she is... in case something happened.

JOHN: You'll have to talk to her.

DAVID: She'd better not be late, that's all.

[He turns to go.]

JOHN: Dad? *[silence]*

DAVID: What? John?

JOHN: Nothing. Sorry.

DAVID: Oh I know I'm fussing, but it's not like our other holidays. We've bought the place. The photographs don't do it justice. We overlook the sea on one side, mountains on the other. There are lemon groves out the back, stretching for miles. It's the real Spain, another world. We'd like to show it to her, to you both. *[pause]* It's so special — stunning.

JOHN: Yes, I know. You said.

DAVID: And it all costs — so.

JOHN: Night, Dad.

DAVID: Right. Thanks. *[David crosses to Jennifer]* You can't say I don't try. What position is that? *[silence]* What do you think about when you're doing Yoga? What are you thinking about now?

[She stops.]

JENNIFER: God.

DAVID: God?

JENNIFER: You remember God, David.

DAVID: Well, vaguely.

JENNIFER: I was wondering if he existed. Do you think God exists?

DAVID: You know what I think.

JENNIFER: When I was a child I believed in God — why did that change?

DAVID: We grow up. We become realists.

JENNIFER: Oh, David, do you really feel so let down?

DAVID: No. I have you. I believe in this family. *[he looks at her. Long pause]*

JENNIFER: What?

DAVID: The Yoga's doing you good.

JENNIFER: I'm looking forward to our holiday.

DAVID: Me too. If God's anywhere, he's in our villa in Spain. Everything packed? I'll strangle Sally.

JENNIFER: You tried Yoga once.

DAVID: Years ago.

JENNIFER: You enjoyed it.

DAVID: I was more supple then. *[exit David]*

[Jennifer crosses to John.]

JENNIFER: Where is she? John?

JOHN: She's alright, that was the message.

JENNIFER: Why does she need to tell us she's alright — unless there was some risk of her not being alright — John?

JOHN: I promised her.

JENNIFER: If you don't tell me, we'll have to call the police. David will. I will. We're worried John — it isn't fair.

[Silence.]

JOHN: She got involved in a riot.

JENNIFER: Sally? In a riot?

JOHN: She's unhurt, it's all over and she's coming home tomorrow.

DAVID: Jennifer? What's going on?

JENNIFER: Nothing. I'm coming now. And you knew?

JOHN: She phoned me afterwards. She's safe, that's what matters, isn't it? There's no need to worry. She just went to watch. That's what she said.

JENNIFER: To watch? Where was it, the Albert Hall?

JOHN: She'll be home tomorrow. *[he turns away]*

JENNIFER: You should have told us.

[Lights fade.]

[Lights rise. The next day.]

DAVID: John! John! We've got twenty minutes before we leave.

[He paces.]

JENNIFER: She'll be here. I've packed her things. All she has to do is get in the car.

DAVID: Have we cancelled the milk?

JENNIFER: No. I'll do it. *[she sits with pen and paper]*

DAVID: And write a note for next door. I'll turn the water off.

JENNIFER: You don't have to.

DAVID: We don't want to come back to a flood.

[Exit David. Enter John. He stands, as if about to speak.]

JENNIFER: Everything alright?

[John nods and leaves. Enter David.]

DAVID: And the dustbins. I'll put them out now.

JENNIFER: They won't come till Tuesday. I'll ask next door to do it.

DAVID: We don't want to impose.

JENNIFER: They're our friends. They'll be glad to.

DAVID: Is the central heating off?

JENNIFER: Yes, but check again if you want.

DAVID: No. *[silence]* You don't think we should call the police?

JENNIFER: She phoned John yesterday to say she was coming.

DAVID: Museums, for three days? Sally?

JENNIFER: John, is your window closed?

JOHN: Yes.

JENNIFER: And take all the plugs out of the sockets — John?

JOHN: Right.

DAVID: Hand luggage. *[he reads the list while she checks the bag]* Camera?

JENNIFER: Yes.

DAVID: Spare flash?

JENNIFER: Yes.

DAVID: Insurance?

JENNIFER: Yes.

DAVID: Traveller's cheques?

JENNIFER: Yes.

DAVID: Separate from purse?

JENNIFER: Yes.

DAVID: Passports?

JENNIFER: Yes.

DAVID: And air tickets?

JENNIFER: One, two, three, four. *[she re-packs the bag]*

DAVID: *[looks at his watch]* We can't leave without her. I mean, without checking she's alright.

JENNIFER: Wait till half past.

DAVID: *[nods]* I like to be there at the check-in time.

JENNIFER: What's this? *[she pulls out a folder of B.R. leaflets]*

DAVID: Just to look through on the plane. It's Richard's

new scheme. He wants me to check it out.

JENNIFER: It's your holiday.

DAVID: He wants to convince everyone that we need a luxury service, a leisure train he calls it. City achievers slide down to Oxford or Bath, spend a lot of money and slide back again — champagne and caviar all the way.

JENNIFER: It's our holiday.

DAVID: It won't take long — just a few ideas.

JENNIFER: Anna Marie.

DAVID: What?

JENNIFER: Her number's scribbled on the back.

DAVID: Yes, she changed flats — just for emergency.

JENNIFER: You should write it in your diary, you might lose it.

[Silence.]

DAVID: You're right of course, I should leave work behind.

JENNIFER: I'll leave it out then.

DAVID: Yes, I'll look out for Sally. *[exits]*

[Enter John.]

JOHN: Mum? Mum?

[Jennifer, caught in her own world for a moment, looks up.]

I can't go with you on holiday. I can't.

JENNIFER: What do you mean you can't?

JOHN: I've got something I must do. Finish.

JENNIFER: We're all packed. We're ready to leave. Now.

JOHN: I know. I spent all night trying to convince myself that it was alright to leave everything behind, but I couldn't. This is more important. I'm sorry.

JENNIFER: What's more important?

[Enter David.]

DAVID: We'll have to call the police, anything might have happened.

JENNIFER: He says he doesn't want to come.

JOHN: I didn't say 'want', I said 'can't'.

DAVID: Can't what?

JENNIFER: He says he 'can't' come with us on holiday.

DAVID: Don't be bloody ridiculous. I've put your bag in the car, it's all packed, we're going.

JOHN: No. I'm not. I don't have to go. I can't go.

[Pause.]

DAVID: We have ten minutes before we leave, John? *[John shakes his head]* Don't shake your head at me. Four months ago we asked if you wanted to come and you said yes. Yes is yes. That's the end of it — you committed yourself — now don't spoil everything, just get your hand luggage and wait in the car.

JOHN: I'm not going. I've made up my mind.

DAVID: You made up your mind? When was this?

JOHN: This morning.

DAVID: Oh, this morning.

JENNIFER: David.

JOHN: I'm sorry — I know that it seems wrong.

DAVID: It doesn't seem wrong. It is wrong. For pity's sake, what's going on? Why can't we just leave for our holiday like any other family, why this?

JOHN: I have to stay here — at the flat.

JENNIFER: What for?

DAVID: It doesn't matter what for, he's made up his mind — this morning.

JOHN: I have to work.

DAVID: Don't be childish, John, you haven't done a day's work since you left the warehouse. You're not at work, you're an Art Student.

JENNIFER: David. Can't you bring your work with you?

DAVID: Take it to the car. I'll take it.

JOHN: It's a ten foot square painting — it's too big.

[Silence.]

DAVID: And that's the reason, for all this?

[Sally enters the house, but not the room.]

JENNIFER: Surely it can wait. Why can't it wait?

JOHN: If I went on holiday, I'd be thinking about the painting all the time — I can't leave it. It possesses me — entirely.

DAVID: Now I've heard it all.

JENNIFER: David.

DAVID: What we have here is a spoilt, selfish, pretentious, middle class brat, and the nauseating thing is, people will think it's our fault.

JENNIFER: David — he's....

DAVID: Stop saying David, I know who I am.

JENNIFER: He's not coming.

DAVID: Two weeks, that's all we ask. Good God, we're not asking, we're giving, isn't that what we always do?

JENNIFER: He's not coming and that's it.

[Enter Sally.]

DAVID: *[he sees Sally]* Well that's something. Your brother isn't coming on holiday. *[pause]* Where have you been? Your mother's been worried sick.

JENNIFER: We'll sort that out later. Sally, I've....

DAVID: I was talking to Sally.

JENNIFER: Will no one listen to me! *[pause]* We'll talk later, we have to leave for the airport now. Sally, your ticket and passport are here, and I've packed your bag, it's in the car, so don't do anything, don't change, just get into the car and we'll leave — Sally?

SALLY: *[she shakes her head]* I'm not coming either... I said I'm not coming either.

ALL:
SONG: *['Paradise']*

SALLY: Just being myself —
JOHN: Roads to freedom —
JENNIFER: Yes, we're going —

ALL: Paradise
Days of healing in Paradise
All our labour rewarded
All our pain set aside
All the love we have hoarded
Spent in learning, forgiving and living
in Tenderness

Four strangers bound by blood
How can we learn to be friends?

DAVID: Sally, please. There's no need to copy John. He's not worth copying.

SALLY: I'm not copying anyone.

DAVID: Sally. This is our holiday. It only comes round once a year, we want to share it with you. Please, Sally, just come with us as arranged.

SALLY: You don't understand....

DAVID: This is ridiculous. *[he laughs]* It's ridiculous! *[exit]*

[John and Jennifer stare at Sally.]

SALLY: I don't want to hear.

JENNIFER: Have you any money? Anything to live off for the next two weeks? Then I'll write you a cheque.

JOHN: You should go.

SALLY: I don't care what you think I should do.

JENNIFER: Tell Mrs Jenkins she needn't water the plants. Tell her that you'll do them. Sally?

SALLY: Yes, yes. I'll water the plants.

[Re-enter David with their luggage which he throws at them.]

DAVID: It's time you woke up. *[to John]* You, from whatever possesses you, God knows what that is, and you, *[to Sally]* from whatever it is that I don't understand — and I'm sure I don't — and I don't care. I really don't care — none of it matters. This holiday mattered. *[he picks up his work from the table]* Do you think I enjoy working on this rubbish? Do you think I do it for my own benefit? *[silence]* We're late. *[exit David]*

JENNIFER: We'll see you in two weeks.

JOHN: I'm sorry.

[She embraces him. Sally makes it clear that she doesn't want to be touched. Exit Jennifer.]

SALLY: What? What? I thought you'd left home. Go on. *[silence]* You think it's alright for you because of some stupid painting.

JOHN: Yes.

SALLY: Well, it isn't.

JOHN: I think it is.

SALLY: You really believe your painting matters? It doesn't. It's nothing. I could put a foot through it and nothing in the world would have changed. Nothing.

JOHN: Yes it would.

SALLY: Don't, just don't do that.

JOHN: I don't know why you came back.

SALLY: Because they'd worry! And I care. *[silence]* I couldn't stay up there could I? This boy asked me what I was doing after the riot and I said "I'm going on holiday". It's a nice house this, isn't it? Our parents are nice too; you come home, ruin their holiday and they pay you for it. Very nice.

JOHN: I've got to go.

SALLY: Don't patronize me.

JOHN: I've work to do.

SALLY: You can't go.

JOHN: I have to finish this painting — I haven't any choice. That's the truth. *[silence]*

SALLY: Can I come? To the flat? I'll make cups of tea — quietly.

JOHN: No. *[she is very hurt]* When I've finished the picture you can have it. I promise.

SALLY: You promised you wouldn't tell them where I'd been, but you did.

JOHN: I'll give you the picture.

SALLY: I don't want it. It's not important. It doesn't matter.

JOHN: Yes it does.

[Lights fade on the two, staring at each other.]

END OF ACT TWO

Act Three

JOHN: *[As narrator.]*

March, 1985. It's Sally's wedding day. In 1984 she met a man several years older than herself called Alan. He runs an advertising agency in London. It's a sunny day.

[Her mother helps her to get dressed.]

SALLY: I'm going to fall.

JENNIFER: Now?

SALLY: No. Not now — going down the aisle.

JENNIFER: Nonsense.

SALLY: I'll get my heel stuck in one of those stupid grills.

JENNIFER: David's asked the vicar to cover them up.

SALLY: I'm not used to heels — I'm going to fall over, I know it.

JENNIFER: You'll be holding on to your Dad.

SALLY: And we'll both fall over. Can you imagine?

JENNIFER: How does that feel?

SALLY: Better. No it's fine. What time is it?

JENNIFER: We've plenty of time, you let us worry about the time.

SALLY: I haven't felt like this since my driving test.

[Jennifer stands back to look at Sally.]

JENNIFER: You passed your driving test. You look beautiful.

SALLY: If you weren't my mother I'd believe you.

JENNIFER: *[returns to the dress]* Have you and Alan talked about children?

SALLY: Only as a means of selling breakfast cereal.

JENNIFER: I'm serious.

SALLY: No, we haven't talked about children. We've too much to do, a business to run.

JENNIFER: As long as you don't rush in.

SALLY: I'm not rushing in — we're getting married to be together, not separated by children.

JENNIFER: Sally!

SALLY: The people I know with children never see each other — mind you they'd all be divorced if they saw each other. How's it doing down under?

JENNIFER: We're getting there.

SALLY: Mind at ease?

JENNIFER: I don't want you to do anything you might regret.

SALLY: Do you regret it then, having us?

JENNIFER: Of course not.

SALLY: What would you have done, if you hadn't — had us?

JENNIFER: I don't know. Become someone else I suppose.

SALLY: I know what we're going to do. Winter snow, summer sun.

JENNIFER: I thought you had a business to run. Turn around.

[Sally spins around.]

SALLY: You see, I shall go to the Ball! *[pause]* Don't worry about me — I'll be alright.

JENNIFER: I've got something for you to wear — something blue. I wore it on my wedding day. It's for luck. *[she gives Sally a blue shell necklace]*

SALLY: It doesn't go does it? Maybe I could wear it round my wrist.

JENNIFER: No, just put it in your bag.

SALLY: I decided against a bag, too much to hold.

JENNIFER: You'll need somewhere for tissues.

SALLY: I'm not going to cry.

JENNIFER: What if you sneeze? *[Sally wipes her nose on her wedding dress. They laugh. Silence]* I'll get the rest of my makeup on. You look beautiful — you'll have to get used to people saying it.

SALLY: Well — if I look beautiful it's your fault.

[Exit Jennifer. Sally practices walking in her high heels. She turns and sees John.]

SALLY: John! *[she embraces him]*

JOHN: Look at you.

SALLY: No, don't look at me. I thought you weren't going to make it.

JOHN: Where's everyone?

SALLY: Dad's fetching the button holes. Mum's upstairs fixing her face. Did you come by train?

JOHN: No, I hitched. High heels too.

SALLY: They're not 'high heels' — an inch, that's all.

JOHN: Another inch and you'd pass for an adult.

SALLY: You. *[they tussle as in Act One]*

JOHN: Is there anything to eat? I'd like something to eat.

SALLY: Mum's made up some sandwiches for 'casual callers'.

[She gives them to him and he eats them hurriedly.]

JOHN: How is she?

SALLY: Mum? She's alright. She's been alright ever since we left home. You should visit more often, then you'd know. Have another sandwich. Mum, John's arrived. She's started going to church. And how are you?

JOHN: Fine, just hungry.

SALLY: I wanted to visit you.

JOHN: I was busy. I can always come over to you, see the new house. What's it like?

SALLY: Incredible.

JOHN: I'll come over then, when you get back. I've brought you something.

[He gives her a painting, wrapped up.]

SALLY: I hope it's one of yours. Shall I open it now?

JOHN: No, when you're alone.

SALLY: Thank you. If I came over, I wouldn't bring Alan. Seems daft, both of us living in London and not seeing each other.

JOHN: I don't mind — if you bring Alan.

[Enter Jennifer.]

JENNIFER: John! *[she kisses him]* Everything alright?

JOHN: Fine.

JENNIFER: Are you hungry? I made some sandwiches.

[She sees the plate with one sandwich left.]

JOHN: They were lovely.

JENNIFER: I'll make some more.

JOHN: No, I've done well.

JENNIFER: You look a bit pale, don't you think, Sally?

SALLY: He's fine.

JENNIFER: It's lovely to have you both home. What's this?

SALLY: Present from John.

JENNIFER: I hope Alan likes it. That's the thing with marriage, you both have to like it or you can't put it on the wall.

SALLY: We'll see about that. *[she walks up and down]*

JENNIFER: She's been practising all week, ever since she tripped over at the rehearsal.

SALLY: You should have seen me. The Dying Swan.

JENNIFER: Her heel got stuck in a grill.

SALLY: I shouldn't have had my head in the oven. *[they laugh at this]* I hate heels.

JENNIFER: David's asked the vicar to put carpet over them.

SALLY: I'm not used to heels. They pinch.

JOHN: Why don't you wear flat shoes?

[She stops.]

SALLY: Alan likes heels —

[Enter David.]

DAVID: John, good to see you. *[sees Sally in her dress for the first time]* Sally, look at you.

SALLY: No, don't. I'll be fine as long as no one looks at me.

DAVID: How are you, John? *[they shake hands]* I've got the buttonholes. We didn't think you were going to make it. Come by train?

JOHN: No, I hitched.

DAVID: You're here, that's the main thing. It's a beautiful day for you, Sally — not a cloud in sight. They should be playing cricket.

JENNIFER: Who?

DAVID: Well, anybody. *[pause]* On a day like this. *[he takes the last of the sandwiches, or tries to]*

JENNIFER: Those were for casual callers.

DAVID: They came in a coach, did they?

SALLY: What's the time?

JENNIFER: Plenty of time.

DAVID: I've just seen the photographer lurking round the church.

JENNIFER: He's early.

DAVID: Are you sure you made the right choice?

JENNIFER: He was recommended.

DAVID: Somehow I don't trust a photographer with a glass eye. *[silence]* He had a glass eye. *[silence]* That's the trouble with the world. No one's gullible any more.

JENNIFER: Are you going to take your camera, just in case?

DAVID: I can't carry it up the aisle. Sally doesn't want to be given away by a tourist.

JENNIFER: Put it in the car.

DAVID: I'm not leaving it in the car. It cost seven hundred quid.

JOHN: I'll carry it.

DAVID: As we say at British Rail "There are no problems, only solutions".

SALLY: What's the matter with you?

JENNIFER: He's got a speech to make.

DAVID: I'm nervous.

SALLY: Well be nervous but stop being such a prat.

[Silence. John laughs, and Jennifer.]

JOHN: I'm sorry.

DAVID: No, go ahead, laugh. I like the sound of it. But you'd better hurry up and get changed, put your suit on.

JOHN: I haven't got a suit.

DAVID: You can't go like that, to a wedding.

JOHN: I don't have a suit.

DAVID: I've got spare suits upstairs, you'll find one to fit, I'm sure.

SALLY: He'd look ridiculous in one of your old suits, they've got flares.

DAVID: They have not. I'd like him to wear a suit, a modern suit.

JENNIFER: It doesn't matter what he wears, David.

DAVID: Of course it matters. It's Sally's day, we make an effort. A suit for one day, is that too much to ask?

SALLY: He's fine as he is.

JOHN: I'll try a suit on, I don't mind.

DAVID: You know where they are.

SALLY: You don't have to try anything on. I don't care what he wears. It's my day and I don't care.

[Silence.]

DAVID: Things don't change do they? Right. Cuff-links. *[exit]*

JENNIFER: Take no notice.

DAVID: Jennifer? Do you know where the cuff-links are?

[Exit Jennifer.]

JOHN: I'm sorry, I didn't think.

SALLY: It doesn't matter. *[silence]* Are you staying here tonight?

JOHN: Yes.

SALLY: Your room's full of my things. I'll clear it out. *[pause]* Dad's taken my room. They're sleeping in separate rooms.

[Silence.]

JOHN: So, what's he like, Alan?

SALLY: I don't know if you'll like him, but you're not going to marry him, so it doesn't matter. *[pause]* I don't want you to say anything. Just be there.

JOHN: I haven't seen you.

SALLY: That's not my fault.

JOHN: I only wanted to ask....

SALLY: Well don't.

JOHN: Why are you getting married?

SALLY: Sod off! I don't have to tell you or anyone else why any more. *[silence]* What are you saying? That I shouldn't get married?

JOHN: No.

[Silence.]

SALLY: Perhaps I don't want to live in some bedsit in South London where I'm ashamed to have visitors. Is that right? Perhaps I don't want to be so hard up I can't afford a train ticket home, or a meal. You're in no position to try and save me, John....

JOHN: I wasn't trying....

SALLY: ...It's not me that needs saving. What are you going to do when you've no money to buy canvas, brushes, paint? Paint in blood? I know what I'm doing, can't you even respect that without asking why? I know why exactly. And if you really wanted to know what Alan's like, why haven't you bothered to come and meet him? He's ambitious, he's organised. He meets artists like you every week, and occasionally he rescues one and in a couple of months they paint pictures that sell, like bloody Michelangelo. But you wouldn't stoop so low as a well paid job. You prefer to suffer. Whatever it is you suffer for I haven't got. What I've got is Alan.

[Enter David.]

DAVID: What's all this?

JOHN: Nothing.

SALLY: John thinks I shouldn't get married, don't you?

[Silence.]

DAVID: Why don't you go back to London, John. Go on, catch a train this time. I'll give you the money.

JOHN: Alright.

SALLY: You're not leaving.

DAVID: You've been here ten minutes. What are you trying to do? Spoil everything? Is that what you want?

SALLY: Leave him alone.

DAVID: I won't allow you to spoil this day.

SALLY: Leave him alone.

[Enter Jennifer carrying a bouquet of flowers for Sally.]

JENNIFER: What's going on?

JOHN: I'd better go.

JENNIFER: Go where?

SALLY: I don't want you to go.

JENNIFER: John?

JOHN: I'm sorry.

DAVID: He told Sally not to get married.

JOHN: I didn't. I asked her why she was getting married. That's all.

DAVID: It amounts to the same thing. *[pause]* It doesn't matter what he says or thinks, not today. It's your day. *[silence]* Look, these things happen in families at these times. It's normal, ordinary. Let's just forget it — get on with the day.

JENNIFER: It's not up to you, David. You don't have to push anything along. Sally?

SALLY: I'm getting married — now.

DAVID: Satisfied? Well, let's have a coffee. There's still time. I think everything's done. My speech is ready, and by popular request I've cut out all references to trains. Except seven.

[This breaks the ice. Sally smiles.]

DAVID: That's better. Coffee then.

JENNIFER: No time, the first car's arrived. That's you and I... John?

[John and Sally hug.]

SALLY: Go on.

JENNIFER: *[gives Sally the bouquet]* Just hand it to the bridesmaid when the rings are exchanged. *[she kisses her and steps back]* You look beautiful.

ALL:
SONG: *['Never Shall Love Dissemble']*

We touch the water, cold and deep,
Where all our fear is sleeping,
Hearing a voice, a voice sing patiently,
"Never shall love dissemble

Love is the richest of all our neighbours
Never shall love dissemble."

JENNIFER: See you at the church. *[exit]*

DAVID: Well — the time draws near. We'll probably have to circle the church a few times to let the stragglers in. Ha! Mr and Mrs Straggler. *[pause]* He's a good man, Sal, I met some of his family. *[pause]*

SALLY: Is the car here?

DAVID: No not yet. When you were a little girl I used to imagine what this moment would be like. This day. It's so odd that it's arrived. Time creeps up. *[silence]* Don't go to many weddings these days. Most of our friends got married in the sixties. Once we had to stand in a circle around the couple who were, well — in the middle — wearing Afghans or Caftans or something, and at the end of the ritual, we had to turn to a complete stranger and say "I love you, peace on earth" Ha! Funny thing is they do the same thing in church these days at the end of Sunday Service. Some churches, so your Mum says. *[pause]* We do love you — I do. Sally?

SALLY: Car's arrived.

[He offers his arm and suddenly all her defences crumble and she embraces him, as a child once more. Then extracting herself, she offers her arm and David takes it. They exit.]

SCENE TWO

[They arrive home at the end of the wedding day. It is twelve o'clock. Jennifer has had too much to drink. She fetches three glasses and a bottle of wine.]

DAVID: Well done everyone. Went off very smoothly. What time is it?

JOHN: Twelve o'clock. I'll get some coffee.

DAVID: A good day's work.

JENNIFER: He's rather ugly isn't he?

DAVID: Who's ugly?

JENNIFER: Alan. His jaw sticks out and he's got piggy eyes.

DAVID: Still, it was a lovely day — some lovely presents.

JENNIFER: He was very pushy, I thought. Pushing himself to the front of every conversation.

DAVID: Still....

JENNIFER: Yes, it was a lovely day. Aren't we allowed to say anything else?

[Enter John with coffee.]

DAVID: Thank you, John. For everything. No, you were a great help in all departments. Even without a suit.

JENNIFER: Here, here!

DAVID: It all went off very well, apart from the parking. Never enough parking spaces at churches. If I were a churchman I'd think seriously about car parks.

JENNIFER: That'd be useful.

DAVID: Well, thanks anyway.

JENNIFER: Here's to John.

DAVID: Cheers. Why don't you stop over tomorrow, have some lunch?

JOHN: *[he looks at his parents]* No, I must get back.

DAVID: Ah! You've got a picture on the go. Half way through I expect. How is work?

JOHN: Good. I feel as if I'm doing some very exciting work. It's good to have time to do what I really want to do — so much time.

DAVID: Well, no need to hitch back. Catch the 125. *[he takes out his wallet]*

JOHN: No. Honestly.

DAVID: I want to give it to you — I know it's not easy in London.

JENNIFER: Take it — it'll make him happy.

JOHN: Thank you.

DAVID: I was talking to Alan, we discussed a common past. *[pause]* His father was a slate miner, did you know that? *[silence]* But after that we disagreed about everything — not unpleasantly, he's very genial. He supported the Falklands war, he didn't support the Miner's Strike. Just wedding talk, I know, still, you have to admire a man like Alan. He believes in himself. I didn't think he was ugly at all.

JENNIFER: I'm going to have a proper drink. *[exit]*

DAVID: We're farming out our advertising to people like Alan. Up and coming agencies. I'm sure Alan's firm could do with an artist of your quality. I thought when they got back from Greece I could speak to him, and Sally would put in a word. If you wanted.

JOHN: Great.

[Enter Jennifer.]

DAVID: I wouldn't mix drinks.

JENNIFER: If I were you. Here's to Sally and Alan. Their future happiness. *[to John]* She does love him you know. *[pause]* But not enough. That's my impression.

DAVID: That's the trouble with mixing drinks.

JOHN: Well, I'm off to bed.

DAVID: Good night then.

JOHN: Night, Mum.

[She raises her glass to him. Exit John.]

DAVID: You drove him away.

JENNIFER: I drove him away?

DAVID: I'm going to bed.

JENNIFER: Don't go to bed, please. Stay down here just a while. *[pause]* I felt such a fool. I spent the whole day fighting back tears.

DAVID: I don't think that's foolish.

JENNIFER: Here's to us. Our future. A country cottage, lots of grandchildren, long vacations.

DAVID: Anything for a long vacation.

JENNIFER: Is life that bad?

DAVID: You know, I think we should sell the villa. I was talking to Alan. He said we should sell up and move further up the coast. Buy a derelict building, do it up and start again. Make a killing.

JENNIFER: Why not? Here's to you and Alan.

DAVID: Jennifer.

JENNIFER: Here's to John and Sally. Here's to me and you. Here's to Anna Marie — the whole family.

END OF ACT THREE

Act Four

SCENE ONE

JENNIFER: *[As narrator.]*

April, 1989. On the table is a small box containing a few personal items belonging to John. David is slowly looking through them. Jennifer enters. She has been walking.

JENNIFER: What is it?

DAVID: A few of John's things. Somebody brought them down. A friend of John's. *[pause]* There's a letter. They found it inside a book.

JENNIFER: A letter to us?

DAVID: No. It's to the Home Secretary of all people.

JENNIFER: Have you read it?

DAVID: Yes.

[Sally nods. Jennifer holds out her hand.]

You don't have to read it now.

JENNIFER: Give it to me.

[He gives her the letter.]

JENNIFER: It's a photocopy.

DAVID: They needed the original for the inquest.

JENNIFER: *[she reads]* "I'm twenty seven years old..." *[she breaks down]*

DAVID: Jennifer, read it later.

JENNIFER: No. You read it. Please. *[pause]* David.

[Sally goes to her room.]

DAVID: *[reads]* "Dear Home Secretary. You probably receive many letters like this but I'd be grateful if you would read to the end because I need to make my situation clear to you. I'm twenty seven years old. For ten years I have striven to do what I thought I was meant to, to add to the cultural life of this country through painting. I'm an artist. Of course one must not only fulfil one's individual desires but contribute to society. I have painted murals for the MSC. I have cleaned the windows of office blocks and drawn on the pavements of shopping malls. However, I have come to rely on state subsidy in order to continue working as a painter.

Nearly a year ago I had an interview at the Job Centre. I was told that there was use for me as a painter and decorator. The office then wrote to me, saying that a doubt had arisen about my availability for work and that my money was suspended. I have also been in protracted negotiations with the Social Security and the council about housing benefit, and the possibility of council housing, although being single I know I am not a priority. It is clear that I won't receive any money for the foreseeable future, money which I have come to regard as the smallest acknowledgement the state could possibly award me. My landlord has given me three weeks to meet my arrears. He says if I will not pay him he will take action, which means eviction.

But I believe I have a solution to his problem and yours."

JENNIFER: Go on.

[David hands her a handkerchief before continuing.]

DAVID: "Please understand, it is nothing to do with lack of

personal love that prompts my action. I'm well aware that my family and friends care deeply for me. It is simply that I don't know how to continue if there is no need for my existence. There is no place for an artist today, only buyers and sellers. I have tried to be honest. I have never cheated, or lied, or stolen, or pretended to be anything I wasn't. I now fully agree that the burden for the tax payer of keeping me alive is neither cost effective nor worthwhile. Perhaps the genetic engineering people could come up with a system whereby such an animal as an artist didn't get born. This would enable society to run more smoothly and save it, and the individuals themselves, the hassle of suicide."

[Lights fade on Jennifer and David. They rise. Jennifer is still sitting but now holds the letter which she stares at. It is several hours later. Sally is still in her room. David approaches her.]

DAVID: Why don't you come downstairs? Have a coffee. there's no point in sitting up here. *[silence]* Sally?

SALLY: I went to see him about five weeks ago. I didn't arrange it because I knew he'd put me off, so I just turned up. He didn't want to let me in at first, but I put my foot in the door. It was a terrible place. There was a mattress on the floor, a sink and a cooker. It hadn't been cleaned for months. He tried to tidy up and offer me a cup of tea, but he couldn't find any milk or sugar *[she almost laughs]* or tea. We talked for a while and he became relaxed. He seemed alright. He said that he felt bad that he'd lied to you about going for job interviews, which he'd given up ages ago, because people didn't want his work. He hated lying — he said he didn't want to hurt you. He was more talkative than I can remember. He didn't seem down at all. He told me he'd decided upon a plan of action. He sounded so positive, but I couldn't help feeling angry towards him, because I found the whole place, him, offensive. Then he asked me why I'd come and I told him to offer him some work with the agency. We needed some figure work that could pass as 'classical' and he said without any anger, that if I wanted to give him money that was fine, but not to pretend that he could work like that. So I did. I gave him some money, and I didn't think about him for about two weeks because he seemed so positive. I didn't see.

[David cannot help her with her private grief.]

ALL:
SONG: *['Tenderness']*

In the house and in the heart,
Every communion is a giving and a receiving
The taste of the food on the table,
And the light, the light in the room,
And the peace, the peace and wholeness
Of the moment,
In the house and in the heart,
And in the love
The taste of the food upon the table
And the tenderness.

JENNIFER: David.

DAVID: Mm?

JENNIFER: I want to send the letter to a newspaper. *[pause]* I want it published.

DAVID: Jennifer....

JENNIFER: I want other people to read it.

DAVID: What do other people matter? We don't know 'other people'. John didn't know 'other people'.

JENNIFER: I'll ask Sally — we'll have to agree.

DAVID: It's not up to Sally, or you. *[pause]* If you want to send it somewhere, send it to the Home Secretary.

JENNIFER: It wouldn't do any good.

DAVID: What good will it do sending it to the bloody newspapers? Maybe we could sell it. *[pause]* I'm sorry. I just don't see that it can serve any purpose, other than to make us into a... 'freak show'.

JENNIFER: We can't keep it to ourselves. It doesn't belong to us.

DAVID: Who does it belong to? Society? You want to blame John's death on Society? *[silence]*

JENNIFER: We loved him. He knows we loved him. He said so. It's not — just to do with us. It's not our fault.

DAVID: No? He didn't hurl himself off a cliff or walk into the sea. He threw himself under a train. A bloody train.

[He breaks down. Jennifer comforts him. Lights fade.]

SCENE TWO

SALLY: *[As narrator.]*

Late September, 1989.

[Jennifer is re-potting some plants. Enter David.]

DAVID: Everything alright?

JENNIFER: Yes. You?

DAVID: *[nods]* I'll be down the other end of the garden then.

JENNIFER: *[she smiles]* Do we need another bonfire, David?

DAVID: *[shrugs]* I've always been a bit of a kid when it comes to bonfires.

[Enter Sally with overnight bag. Jennifer works throughout the scene.]

JENNIFER: Sally! *[they greet each other]* Your Dad's in the garden, he'll be here in a minute. Journey alright?

SALLY: The second class carriages were heaving so I sat in the first class and paid the extra.

JENNIFER: I don't blame you. Do you want a cup of tea?

SALLY: No thanks, I had some on the train.

JENNIFER: I'd just like to finish these.

SALLY: You go ahead. I'll take my bag up.

JENNIFER: I've made up your room. *[exit Sally]* Are you sure you won't have tea?

SALLY: Yes, I'm sure.

[Sally drops her bag in her room. Before returning to Jennifer she stops outside John's room and looks in.]

JENNIFER: Alright?

SALLY: I see you've cleaned John's room.

JENNIFER: Yes. You don't mind?

SALLY: No, of course not.

JENNIFER: It seemed wrong, just to leave it. *[silence]* You look very smart.

SALLY: I had a meeting this morning.

JENNIFER: I don't know how you do it, rushing from place to place.

SALLY: It's exciting.

JENNIFER: It would have to be. *[pause]* David and I were worried. You usually plan these visits so far in advance.

SALLY: I do have some news.

JENNIFER: Oh?

SALLY: Nothing bad. Good news. But it can wait till Dad comes in — I don't want to say the same thing twice.

JENNIFER: *[calling]* David! David! He's made a bonfire — David! He gets lost in his own world these days. *[Jennifer returns to her work]*

SALLY: How are you both?

JENNIFER: Getting through. We thought of going on a long holiday to India.

SALLY: India!

JENNIFER: Yes, I know. We looked at all the brochures and decided on something different. I'm going to wash in the Ganges.

SALLY: If there's room between all the dead bodies.

JENNIFER: Sally!

SALLY: It's true. When are you going?

JENNIFER: We thought we'd go for Christmas. We didn't think we should stay here — anyway, we'll miss the worst of the winter. *[silence]* We sold the villa, did we tell you?

SALLY: No.

JENNIFER: To a holiday firm. That's how we can afford the trip. I'm sorry, we should have told you about the villa.

SALLY: There's no need. I never got there, remember?

[Silence. Enter David. He has also been gardening.]

DAVID: Sally, Sally. How are you? *[he kisses her]*

SALLY: I'm very well.

DAVID: You look as if there's an occasion round the corner.

JENNIFER: She's been to a meeting.

DAVID: How was the journey?

SALLY: First class. *[she smiles at Jennifer]*

DAVID: Ah — I see.

SALLY: I thought you hated gardening.

DAVID: Well, it grows on you. Ha! No, well, your Mother needed a hand, so — cup of tea?

JENNIFER: She says she's got some news.

[David looks expectant, thinking that she is going to have a baby.]

SALLY: Right. I'm going to open a new branch of the agency out of town, out of London.

DAVID: That's marvellous. Where?

SALLY: Here. We're only one and a half hours from London, if that. Property's cheaper, and the docklands are being re-developed, new business is moving in, who'll need advertising. It's the perfect place.

DAVID: Of course it is. I'm surprised no one's done it before.

SALLY: They have. There's a lot of competition, but nothing we can't overcome.

DAVID: Well, competition's healthy —

JENNIFER: So they say.

[Silence.]

DAVID: That is good news. When does it all start?

SALLY: It already has. I'm going to look for office space next week.

DAVID: Next week? Sally, why didn't you say? I could have done something.

JENNIFER: David.

SALLY: No, I'll need some help.

DAVID: The old warehouse space is going pretty fast.

British Rail are letting out old station houses to small businesses. I'll see what's around. We'll find somewhere. And you'll need to find a flat, or a house pretty central — I could have gone round the estate agents for you if I'd known.

SALLY: I'm starting the business on my own, so I thought if I could stay here until I got things moving...? Alan's staying in London to keep everything ticking over.

DAVID: Of course you can stay. Well that's even better. Stay as long as you want, you know that, and Alan, whenever he wants.

SALLY: Thanks. If he's not busy. You know what he's like.

DAVID: That's why he's successful. I think this deserves a toast.

SALLY: Not for me — I've given it up.

DAVID: Oh. Jenny?

JENNIFER: Yes, I'll join you.

[Exit David.]

SALLY: You don't mind me staying? It is alright?

JENNIFER: It won't be easy.

SALLY: I don't have to stay.

JENNIFER: That's not what I said. David's here most of the time. We're not used to it. We don't always get on. He doesn't go out much.

SALLY: What about you?

JENNIFER: I've never walked so far in my life! *[pause]* I want you to stay, of course. I'm just saying, it won't be easy.

SALLY: It never was.

JENNIFER: So, where's Alan?

SALLY: I don't know. Abroad somewhere. *[pause]* I don't really care.

JENNIFER: You should have told me.

SALLY: What could you have done?

JENNIFER: Are you alright?

SALLY: Oh yes. I bought some designer armour.

[Silence.]

JENNIFER: Where's the money coming from then?

SALLY: Oh, it's Alan's money, as much as I can get. It's part of our deal. And we've landed a healthy contract with an ecology agency who want to prick people's consciences with pictures of dying whales. So we're all set for six months. After that, I'll buy Alan out if I can. I'll be rich.

JENNIFER: Is that what you want?

[Silence.]

SALLY: I'll be able to look after the house over Christmas.

JENNIFER: Do you think that's a good idea?

SALLY: I could always come to India with you. Dad wouldn't mind.

JENNIFER: No! The last thing I want on holiday is another woman — even you.

SALLY: Well said!

[Enter David.]

DAVID: Right. Here's to Sally and the new business.

[They drink.]

SALLY: Mum says you're going to India.

DAVID: Yes, out of the blue, really.

JENNIFER: Not exactly. I've always wanted to go.

DAVID: She's still following the Beatles.

JENNIFER: *[quietly]* You could follow worse.

DAVID: Well, I'll get on.

SALLY: Is there anything I can do to help?

JENNIFER: This needs re-potting, but you'll have to get changed.

DAVID: I've got some spare overalls in the garage.

SALLY: No, too much trouble. I'll watch the telly in my room. Relax a bit.

DAVID: Fine.

JENNIFER: We'll eat about six.

[Exit Sally to her room. They work for a moment, then Jennifer stops, unable to continue. David comforts her.]

DAVID: I love you.

THE END

In The Bleak Midwinter

Notes to the Original Production

In the Bleak Midwinter was first performed on Wednesday, 19th September, 1990 at Albert Road Methodist Church and Community Centre, Penarth, South Glamorgan.

Cast

Zac..Richard Berry
Miriam..Erica Eirian
Mak...Peter Rumney
Gill...Helen Gwyn

Directed by..........................Rosamunde Hutt
Designed by...........................Richard Aylwin
Music by..................................Paula Gardiner
Lighting Design and
Stage Management.................. Ian Buchanan

1. The play was performed in the round, and began with the sound of a cold wind blowing. The cast entered and sang the first verse of 'In The Bleak Midwinter', arranged by Paula Gardiner. At the end of the song, the actor playing Mak addressed the audience with these words:

   Ladies and Gentlemen
   Once upon a time
   Somewhere in the Black Mountains
   Not far from Bethlehem

2. At the end of the first act, the same actor, now in the role of the king, addressed the audience with these words:

   Ladies and Gentlemen
   I shall now count to seven at the end of
   which there will be a short interval.
   Don't worry, it's an old trick of the East.
   1...2...3...4...5...6...7.

   As he counted, he raised his arms and the house lights rose.

3. The shepherds were conceived of as being late nineteenth century in dress.

4. At the 'tossing in a blanket scene', an improvised section resulted in the following action. They decide to toss Mak in a blanket. In the action previous to this, Miriam has given her baby to a member of the audience to look after. Zac enquires of Mak meanwhile how old he is in order to determine the number of bumps he should be given. Mak lies and says seventeen, then corrects himself to thirty-five. After some tomfoolery, Mak lies down in the blanket, and the characters of Gill and Zac get hold of two corners each, and count 'one', and look into the air as if Mak was being tossed high to the ceiling, as which point they freeze in time. At this point Miriam realises she has put the baby down somewhere and shouts "Where's my baby?" She finds it amongst the audience and returns. The others come back to life and say loudly "thirty-five", as if they have tossed Mak that many times. They are exhausted from such activity, with broken backs, and Mak has had a pleasant time of it. The action then returned to the script.

5. The songs as written by Paula Gardiner, words by Charles Way via the Bible, are a mixture of Jazz and Gospel (this does not include the two carols).

   The first, 'Though Shalt Not Steal' was led by Zac.
   The second, 'Thou Shalt Not Commit Adultery' was led by Miriam.
   The third, 'Song of Ramah' was sung by the two women.
   The lullaby sung by Miriam in Act One, which Gill tries to join in, and the lullaby sung by Mary and Miriam in Act Two are the same tune, which is of a Jewish flavour.

Act One
SCENE ONE

[Somewhere in the Black Mountains. The sound of a cold wind blowing. The cast enter and sing the first verse of 'In The Bleak Midwinter'.]

SONG: In the Bleak Midwinter
Frosty winds made moan,
Earth stood hard as iron,
Water like a stone,
Snow had fallen, snow on snow,
Snow on snow, snow on snow
In the Bleak Midwinter
Long ago.

[At the end of the song, the actor playing Mak steps forward and addresses the audience.]

MAK: Ladies and gentlemen
Once upon a time
Somewhere in the Black Mountains
Not far from Bethlehem.

[Mak exits. Miriam and Zac are huddled round a fire. Miriam with a baby.]

MIRIAM: Zac. Zac.

ZAC: Uh?

MIRIAM: Zac? *[she kicks him]*

ZAC: What?

MIRIAM: Something out there. In the dark.

ZAC: Ssh then.

[She goes and looks — returns.]

ZAC: Can't see nothing. 'Cept the stars. Look at them stars, Miriam. Look at them stars.

MIRIAM: Oh shut up, you daft ol' piece of leather. I heard something. I'm sure of it.

ZAC: Could 'ave been those three over there — drinkin'. You know what they're like when they've 'ad a drop o' drink.

MIRIAM: Hooves?

ZAC: Hooves?

MIRIAM: Horses! Horses mean soldiers.

ZAC: What would soldiers want up 'ere? In the dead o' night — with shepherds?

[Silence.]

MIRIAM: I'm 'alf frozed.

ZAC: Move nearer the fire then.

MIRIAM: Oh I could sit on top of 'un I suppose.

ZAC: Come by me then — I'll warm up the other 'alf. Come, wife.

MIRIAM: "Wife" is it now?

ZAC: Aye "wife" — "husband". *[he smiles]*

MIRIAM: Get awf!

ZAC: It would keep us warm.

MIRIAM: What would?

ZAC: The sheep huddle together — to keep 'em from the wind — so should we.

MIRIAM: I am no sheep!

[He lies back down.]

Don't turn yer back on me. Just cold that's all. Don't feel like nothing... else.

ZAC: *[nods]* We'll be warm enough tomorrow night. We'll find a tidy inn in Bethlehem and spend the night in a bed, with sheets. Ah Hah! Like King an' Queen us'll be tomorrow night.

MIRIAM: Bah. Bethlehem. Don't see why us 'as to go at all.

ZAC: To register.

MIRIAM: Oh, "Register".

ZAC: To enrol.

MIRIAM: "Enrol and Register". What about "to pay yer Poll Tax".

ZAC: It's the law.

MIRIAM: Oh the law — and it wouldn't do for a man to break a law.

ZAC: You 'as to keep the law or nothing at all.

MIRIAM: It's a wrong law — it's an upside down, back to front, downright unfair law, and we shouldn't go.

ZAC: Then there would be soldiers up here. Is that what you want?

MIRIAM: Oh go to sleep, you daft ol' pig's bladder.

ZAC: How can I go to sleep with the sound of your voice ringing round the hills like a cathedral bell.

MIRIAM: You leave my voice out of it. There's nothing wrong wi' my voice.

ZAC: 'Cept that it's always complaining.

MIRIAM: Why shouldn't I? I got grounds.

ZAC: Because it's not noble.

MIRIAM: NOBLE? Oh I suppose it's very noble to get yerself evicted from yer dwelling, and yer wife and babe, pushed out on the common ground in the dead of winter with nothing but a blanket between them and a hell that's as cold as Hell is hot.

ZAC: That weren't my fault.

MIRIAM: 'Course it were your fault. You opened your big noble jaws —

ZAC: He was doing wrong.

MIRIAM: He was the landlord, doing wrong is his rightful business.

ZAC: 'Twas a matter of principle.

MIRIAM: Oh PRINCIPLE. *[she spits]* You got more principles than you 'ave sheep! And both are a mangy lot.

ZAC: They are not!

MIRIAM: Why can't you be like any other poor man who can't afford principles — you 'ave made us paupers with 'em. You got no more sense in you than the sheep, that is my confirmed opinion.

ZAC: That's no hurt to me, sheep are fine, noble creatures.

MIRIAM: Baa — Baa.

ZAC: Who be not as stupid as people rumour.

MIRIAM: Baa — Baa. Oh, he stands up to defend his sheep, very noble, you daft ol' dung bucket.

ZAC: That is not respectful, Miriam!

MIRIAM: I am cold, I am hungry — and I am brim full of hate — so sit down with yer "Miriam".

[He sits.]

ZAC: Miriam, my wife, when the good weather comes you will like it here....

MIRIAM: I don't want no good weather talk.

ZAC: We must must simply bide our time.

MIRIAM: You bide 'em, I'll suffer 'em. It keeps me warm.

ZAC: Look — I have a plan.

MIRIAM: The Garden of Eden you said.

ZAC: Listen... six rams from up 'ere, Welsh hardy stock, and mix 'em with lowland ewes —

MIRIAM: Oh leave off your plans, Zac. I've heard more of your plans than there are stars in the sky. You're a dreamer!

ZAC: Aye, a man who don't dream sees nothing.

MIRIAM: Pardon?

ZAC: I sez a man....

MIRIAM: I heard you. Load of ol' droppings that is. There's more to life than looking up and dreaming.

ZAC: There's more to life than bitter complaint!

MIRIAM: We be both agreed then. There is more to life!

[Silence.]

MIRIAM: *[gently]* Oh, Zac, Zac. Why don't we go back down — live in the town?

ZAC: It would be the death of me. You know it.

MIRIAM: Won't this be the death of all of us? *[pause]* You could do other jobs like... like....

ZAC: Like what? My family have been shepherding these hills since the days of Noah — it's a craft that 'as been handed down to me.

MIRIAM: Why aren't you any good at it then?

ZAC: I am the finest shepherd on these hills, and all who knows me, knows it.

MIRIAM: You reckon a fine shepherd is one who loves his sheep, and whose sheep traipse around after him dewy-eyed....

ZAC: I have a special relationship with my sheep! — and am proud of it.

MIRIAM: Aye. I've never seen a man weep so at the sight of a lamb going to market. They laugh at you.

ZAC: Let 'em laugh. I kill 'em with care — that's my way — I have never shirked my duty when it came to the knife.

MIRIAM: Buy 'em, breed 'em, butcher 'em — and do it fast — that's the way to make a good living.

ZAC: That's as may be.

MIRIAM: What does that mean?

ZAC: As long as we be honest, and true....

MIRIAM: And good?

ZAC: Aye and good — all things will come our way. Us'll prosper and thrive.

MIRIAM: And how will it come our way? Where's all this prosperity and thriving coming from?

ZAC: I don't know — all I know is we've got to wait.

MIRIAM: Oh well, that cheers me up no end. I'll sit and wait!

ZAC: "Yet a little while and the wicked will be no more, though you look well at his place he will not be there."

MIRIAM: So if I look long enough at you, you'll disappear!

ZAC: "But the meek shall possess the land and delight themselves in abundance."

MIRIAM: Bah!

ZAC: *[sadly]* Oh, Miriam.

MIRIAM: Don't say Miriam like that! You and yer head full of turds and wishful thinking.

[Silence.]

ZAC: Don't cry.

MIRIAM: I'm not crying. It's the wind in me eyes, and the cold.

ZAC: Perhaps a bit o' bread in our stomachs would make us feel more like husband and wife.

MIRIAM: No. 'Tis saved for the journey to Bethlehem — I have planned it all out.

ZAC: *[sits and stares at the sky]* Look! — look, a great big potato comin' out of the sky.

MIRIAM: What?

ZAC: There it is. *[he plucks it out]* Oh. *[he tastes it]* Beautifully roasted. Oh, and look there, a string of grapes tumbling from the heavens. Oh... Oh... I am... bursting... and see, suet pudding.

MIRIAM: Oh stop it, stop it, you daft ol' maggot!

ZAC: Why? I'm nearly full.

MIRIAM: 'Cos it's torture!

ZAC: Ah — I couldn't eat another mouthful.

MIRIAM: You're scatty, crazed, head full of worms. *[silence]* What's that sound? I heard a sound. Go and see. Go on.

[He goes. She takes a bit of bread and eats it hungrily.]

ZAC: Nothing out there, 'cept ice and snow, and... What are you eating?

MIRIAM: Me fingernails. What's left of 'em.

SCENE TWO

[A sound.]

MIRIAM: What's that?

ZAC: I heard it too.

MIRIAM: We be murdered now, all 'cos of you.

ZAC: Be still. Who's there? Show yerself!

MAK: *[from the darkness]* 'Tis only I. Mak.

ZAC: *[to Miriam]* Mak.

MIRIAM: *[to Zac]* Which Mak?

ZAC: Which Mak?

MAK: *[from the darkness]* Why Mak. You knows — Mak.

ZAC: *[to Miriam]* You knows, Mak.

MIRIAM: The sheep stealer?

ZAC: The sheep stealer?

MAK: *[from the darkness]* No, not that Mak. I'm the other Mak, not the sheep stealer.

ZAC: *[to Miriam]* Not the sheep st....

MIRIAM: I heard. *[shouts]* Clear awf out of it. You hear me.

MAK: I be returning from Bethlehem, an' me legs 'ave reached the end of their journey, the rest of me is willing, but me legs be in revolt. I will approach.

MIRIAM: You will not, sheepstealer.

[Mak walks into the camp.]

MIRIAM: Zac, stop him.

ZAC: Um —

[Mak takes his hand.]

MAK: Zac!

ZAC: Mak!

MIRIAM: What are you thinking of? Let go his hand.

[Mak continues to shake vigorously.]

He is the sheepstealer.

MAK: I tell ee, Zac, 'tis a curse to be so named and live under the burden of a lie. 'Ave I yet been hung for stealing sheep? Do ee see a mark about my neck? Zac?

ZAC: I see no mark, Mak.

MAK: An' I reckon if a man be innocent before the law, he be innocent before his friend.

ZAC: Aye, I reckon.

MIRIAM: We are not your friends. Get out of this camp.

MAK: You keep a fine camp, Miriam.

MIRIAM: Don't call me Miriam.

MAK: And a fine fire an' all, Zac.

ZAC: Thankee. Come near the fire, Mak.

MIRIAM: Get away from that fire.

ZAC: Miriam.

[Zac and Miriam go to one side.]

MIRIAM: Leave go of me!

ZAC: I will speak.

MIRIAM: Do ee take me for a clod of turf? He 'ave come to rob us.

ZAC: I will fetch word from him that he will not.

MIRIAM: His word is not worth spit! *[she spits]*

ZAC: It be worth summat to me.

[He approaches Mak.]

ZAC: Mak.

MAK: Zac — share the fire with me.

ZAC: Yer most kind.

MIRIAM: What do ee mean "most kind"? It's our fire.

ZAC: Mak.

MAK: Zac.

ZAC: I will 'ave yer word that there will be no sheep stolen here from us this night.

MAK: A poor man don't steal from another poor man. If he do, how shall poor men ever prosper?

ZAC: Yer word.

MAK: Indeed I did count yer sheep as I came in. There be forty-seven now and there shall be forty-seven when I leave.

MIRIAM: What's he doing counting our sheep?

ZAC: You 'ave miscounted. We 'ave forty-eight.

MAK: Ah! Of all the poor men in these winter hills, you be the man I respect most, Zac. Not least for yer summin' up.

ZAC: 'Tis good enough.

MIRIAM: Good enough?

MAK: Miriam.

MIRIAM: Mrs Williams to you.

MAK: May the lord strike me dead this moment if I lie. I have never stolen a sheep in my entire life.

[There is a moment where since Mak is not struck down, he proves that he tells the truth, but in the next instant he collapses, then returns to life.]

[Zac laughs.]

MAK: A jest!

ZAC: A joke.

MIRIAM: And a gibbet for your neck with any luck!

ZAC: Miriam, there be a code of hospitality in these hills which I be mindful of.

MIRIAM: Why us? There be three shepherds over yonder, who 'ave drink enough.

MAK: Drink? Aye, a drink. I have brought a jug of cider from Bethlehem.

ZAC: Cider?

MAK: Aye, mun. And a fine cider it be, made from the sweetest apples in all 'Ereford! Share it with me, both.

[Miriam turns away.]

ZAC: It is not honourable to refuse.

MIRIAM: I never made no claims to be honourable.

[Zac and Mak drink.]

ZAC: Thankee.

MAK: 'Tis a pleasure.

ZAC: Indeed.

[He offers a second glass.]

MIRIAM: That's enough. That stuff'll take yer crook from under ee. How then shall ee run to catch a thief?

MAK: Aye, they don't call it a drop of 'wobbly' for nothing, Zac.

[The men laugh. Mak warms himself.]

Oh, I were wet through. You see this cloak, Zac?

ZAC: I see it — just.... *[he laughs]*

MIRIAM: For pity's sake, can you not hold one glass of cider?

ZAC: Forgive my wife, she have sharpened all her senses except one — her humour.

[Stung by this, Miriam retreats.]

MAK: This cloak, Zac, is all I have against the world. The snow 'ave slept on it, the frost 'ave frozen it and the rain 'ave just plain ignored it. This cloak is as meaningless as life itself.

ZAC: Life is not meaningless, Mak. Life is full of meaning, as the sky is full o' stars.

MIRIAM: Oh my God!

MAK: Aye, Zac, you be a man of the stars. But I look up and I don't see 'em. I see only darkness. In truth, if death were to tip his cap at me I would not flinch, for in death there is no hunger.

ZAC: Aye. Come then, Mak, break some bread with me.

MIRIAM: No.

ZAC: Miriam.

MIRIAM: You leave the bread be.

ZAC: This man 'ave shared with us, an' we must share with him.

MIRIAM: Can you not see his every move as I do?

ZAC: If I lose trust in my fellow man, I lose everything. Give me the bread.

MIRIAM: No — 'tis for our journey to Bethlehem and shall not be touched.

[Mak sees that Zac and Miriam have come to an impasse.]

MAK: Oh what a place Bethlehem is. A regular ants' nest. People arriving from all over the country. Some on foot, some on donkeys, and a few on camels. Why, the whole world is in Bethlehem, seems to me. An' there be soldiers on every corner.

ZAC: Soldiers?

MAK: Aye, the finest dressed soldiers you ever saw. An' in the market place a recruiting officer handing out silver coins to those who'll join Herod's army. I was in 'alf a mind to do so, but I have my Gill to think on. Sweet Gill — she 'ave kept me from kissing the sergeant yet again. *[he laughs]*

MIRIAM: To Hell with Gill, to Hell with you, to Hell with Herod an' all.

MAK: I 'ope you will not say so in such a voice in Bethlehem. They say the dungeons of Herod's palace are only seen once.

[Silence.]

However, while I were in Bethlehem, I saw this *[he shows them a small carved sheep]* an' I thought of yer newly born babe up here on the moor, an' that I should pass through yer camp on my journey home, an' how pleasant it would be to give such a gift and see the baby's face light up. 'Tis beautifully carved. In willow. See I steal no sheep. I do give sheep — for the baby to play with.

ZAC: Take it, Miriam.

MIRIAM: I don't want it.

ZAC: You cannot refuse it. You cannot.

MIRIAM: I will owe this man nothing.

ZAC: Then I accept it with thanks.

MAK: Have ee named the child?

ZAC: No, we are in some disagreement over the name.

MAK: Call him Mak — and I shall be his Godfather.

MIRIAM: Hah!

ZAC: Forgive my wife.

MAK: You are a hard woman, Mrs Williams.

MIRIAM: I am what I have to be.

[Zac gazes distractedly at the carved sheep.]

MAK: And yet beautiful, despite the hardness in you.

MIRIAM: Will you stop him!

ZAC: What?

MAK: I was saying how beautiful yer wife be, Zac.

[Zac looks at Miriam.]

Despite the blueness of her nose, the depth of her frown and the downward shape of her lips. She is beautiful and I can see why you took her for a wife.

ZAC: Why?

[Miriam kicks him.]

Ow!

[Mak closes his eyes in a kind of trance.]

MAK: Her eyes are like doves,
Her hair is like a flock of goats,
Moving down the slopes of Gilead,
Her teeth are like a flock of shorn ewes,
Her lips are like a scarlet thread
And her mouth is lovely.

MIRIAM: Stop it, you hear!

MAK: Her cheeks are like halves of a pomegranate.

MIRIAM: Will you make him stop.

ZAC: Mak.

MAK: Her breasts are like —

ZAC: Mak. Mak.

[He shakes Mak. Mak comes out of his "trance".]

MAK: Zac! Oh, Zac — I was in another world — but it's

good to be back, Zac. Miriam.

MIRIAM: Don't call me Miriam. You're a thief, a liar, a wastrel, a good for nothing —

ZAC: Miriam!

[They turn. Mak has sat down with his hat over his eyes. Silence.]

We must sleep — we have a long journey tomorrow.

MIRIAM: I'll not sleep with him 'ere. I'll not shut eye with him 'ere.

ZAC: As you will woman. Goodnight, Mak.

MAK: Goodnight, Zac. Sleep well. Sleep well.

MIRIAM: I'm watching you.

[Zac falls asleep and Miriam watches Mak. She tries to keep awake but falls to sleep. Mak gets up and finds what he can to steal. As he steals, the others burst into life, singing even as they are being robbed. He steals the blanket from Zac's back, but cannot get at the food which Miriam keeps close to her. At the height of the song, he steals a sheep.]

SONG: You shall not
You shall not, no
You shall not,
You shall not steal
You shall not steal — No
steal — No
steal — No
steal — No
Or be greedy for unjust gain — No
gain — No
gain — No
Nor shall you
No you shall not
You shall not

You shall not rob from the poor
For the poor are the people of the lord (x3)
For the poor are the people
And the lord, he commands
Listen to his commandments
You shall not
No, you shall not
You shall not
You shall not steal!

SCENE THREE

[Mak goes back to his hovel where Gill has been waiting three days.]

MAK: Gill. Gill.

GILL: Who is it?

MAK: It's me. Mak. Who do you think? Let me in.

GILL: Why should I?

MAK: What?

GILL: You have got some cheek.

MAK: None that be not frostbitten, so open up and let me in the warm.

GILL: Three days you've been gone.

MAK: Aye.

GILL: Oh, I'll be back in five minutes he says, and three days later back he comes in the middle of the night.

MAK: Ssh. I was taken on sudden business — to Bethlehem.

GILL: I did not know if you were dead or alive.

MAK: I'm alive, and look — look what I have brought you.

[He gives blanket. She peeps at the blanket.]

GILL: Smells of mutton.

MAK: And a jug of cider.

GILL: 'Alf a jug.

MAK: And I 'ave something else, that'll make yer 'art sing.

[She lets him in.]

GILL: What?

MAK: Da! Da! *[He brings out the sheep.]*

GILL: Oh, Mak, Mak, this is no ordinary stealing, this is a hanging offence.

MAK: I risk my life then. A braver thief there never was.

GILL: Your life? What of my life?

MAK: Oh! *[good-naturedly]* Who cares about life? Does this lamb bleat about life? No, even as he is about to leave it... he lives it to the full. I am a lamb at heart.

GILL: You promised me.

MAK: When did you last eat lamb?

GILL: Twelve month or more.

MAK: Aye! Are we not as good as those flea-bitten keepers of sheep? Shall we not eat as they eat? Come let us to the slaughter.

GILL: Which keepers of sheep?

MAK: You knows the fool on the hill. Zac!

GILL: Zac and Miriam? You stole a sheep from Miriam?

MAK: Aye — from Miriam, not from Herod!

GILL: She is tenfold more terrible than Herod. She will take us straightway to the magistrates, if she do not hang us herself.

[Mak raises the knife.]

MAK: I care not about Miriam.

GILL: You cannot kill it now. *[she tries to stop him]*

MAK: I shall kill it — 'an eat it raw at this rate.

GILL: Yer hunger will betray us, Mak. You must go back.

MAK: Go back? Does the fox go back to sleep in the chicken coop? I will not go back.

GILL: Be quick, before they awake, and when they wake you shall be sleeping at their side, so no suspicion will fall on you when they do count their sheep.

MAK: *[considers]* Aye — Aye. It's a tidy reckoning.

GILL: Go then, and as they wake tell 'em I have given birth this night to a baby boy.

MAK: Right! *[he stops and turns]* Why?

GILL: 'Tis best to have a second plan if the first fails. Go on — before they wake.

SCENE FOUR

[Mak Goes back to the camp fire, as he approaches, Zac wakes up.]

ZAC: Mak?

MAK: Zac, sweet Shep!

ZAC: Are you leaving?

MAK: Aye. I shall trespass on yer goodness no longer.

ZAC: 'Tis no trespass.

MAK: I thankee, but I 'ave 'ad a dream, a most unpleasant dream that drives me fast home.

ZAC: A man must listen to his dreams.

MAK: Aye. I dreamt that my Gill were fat with child an' 'ave tonight brought forth a baby boy.

ZAC: Can't be so, Mak, for I saw yer Gill but a month ago at market selling beads, and she 'ad no lump on 'er.

MAK: So it is with poor women an' poor babies, when both be underfed. I thankee once again. You are a good man.

ZAC: I'm glad my faith in you be rewarded, for I would 'ave taken it personal if you 'ad stolen from me since I 'ad yer word.

MAK: I am yer honest friend.

ZAC: Reformed then?

MAK: Aye. Reformed is the word. It is your goodness and generosity that 'ave reformed me. I shall never steal again. Goodbye.

ZAC: Mak?

MAK: Yes, Zac.

ZAC: That's my crook.

MAK: Aye, so it be, an' it's a fine crook. It works well.

ZAC: Thank you for — for testing it!

MAK: Goodbye, Zac.

ZAC: Goodbye, Mak.

[Mak exits. Miriam wakes with a start.]

MIRIAM: Where's Mak to? Zac. Zac.

ZAC: Gone.

MIRIAM: Gone? You 'ave no more sense than a gap in the hedge. What do ee mean, gone?

ZAC: All's well. I woke an' saw him off. He took no sheep with him, though from sheer habit of theft he took my crook, but I out thought him.

MIRIAM: Why would he go empty handed? 'Tis not natural.

ZAC: He has some dream that Gill were to give birth to a baby boy.

MIRIAM: Count the sheep. *[she kicks him]* Go on.

SCENE FIVE

[Mak arrives back at the hovel.]

MAK: Fear not, it's only me.

GILL: What end did ee make with the shepherds?

MAK: They will 'ave no suspicions of me now, for I was there when Zac woke. Now let us kill it. A bowl for the blood.

GILL: Be soft with her.

MAK: Straight through the eye — into the brain is 'ow the shepherds kill — 'tis over in a moment.

GILL: But first cut off the ear — so there be no mark of Zac's.

[He is about the kill the sheep.]

MAK: To Hell with his ear — I shall eat it.

ZAC: Mak, be you in there?

MAK: By heaven, the turds are fleet of foot.

MIRIAM: Open the door, Mak.

GILL: Give me the lamb.

MIRIAM: Or I will kick it down.

GILL: Hold yer breath, we 'ave a sleeping babe, newly born in here.

MIRIAM: Or shall I put a torch to yer hovel an' smoke ee out?

ZAC: Miriam, there shall be no violence.

[Miriam kicks him.]

[Gill lays down Zac's blanket, covering the baby.]

GILL: But please come in — though guests were unexpected at this hour. Sing. Sing!

MAK: Sing?

GILL: For yer life!

[Mak sings a lullaby, and this is the scene which greets Zac and Miriam as they enter. Miriam gives the baby to Zac and searches.]

MIRIAM: Where's our lamb?

MAK: You 'ave not lost the little lamb I gave ee?

MIRIAM: You know well enough the lamb I mean. Before you came we had forty-eight, including a lamb, now we 'ave forty-seven.

MAK: As I did say, I only counted forty-seven as I came upon yer camp.

MIRIAM: You stop yer lying gums. I'll hear none of it.

MAK: Zac.

ZAC: I did tell 'er you left empty handed, but if we may search to ease our minds.

MAK: Aye search, you'll find nothing here, for that is all we own.

[Miriam searches.]

ZAC: Gill, 'ow be you?

GILL: Oh well — sore, but well.

ZAC: I see yer dream had substance, Mak.

MAK: Aye, a man must listen to his dreams. I'll call him Zac, you can be his Godfather.

ZAC: I thankee.

[Gill groans as the lamb kicks her.]

You hear that, Miriam, I'm a proud Godfather.

MAK: This babe 'ave broken her body in two — 'tis fortunate that we be men, Zac, and be free of such rigours.

GILL: Ow. Ow. *[smiles]* We should celebrate his birth — ow — ow — with our guests.

MAK: Aye, some cider.

MIRIAM: No more cider! An' none of yer false pleasantries neither.

GILL: What ails ee, Miriam? Is ought amiss?

MIRIAM: A missing more like.

ZAC: Hah!

MIRIAM: Shut up!

MAK: No cider, no jokes, it's a hard hearth you keep, Miriam.

MIRIAM: It'll be harder yet, when we find our stolen lamb.

GILL: What — stolen, from under your noses, as you slept? Lord, what a thief that were.

MIRIAM: *[she turns on Mak]* Aye, an' if we catch him how shall we do justice?

MAK: Let him bounce on the end of a rope, that's as I say. A curse on all thieves.

MIRIAM: *[to Zac]* Remember that.

[Gill groans as Miriam gets close.]

MAK: Hark, how Gill does groan.

GILL: Oh my middle.

MAK: Yer 'arts should melt.

ZAC: We should leave.

MIRIAM: I will not leave without my lamb.

[Gill groans.]

MAK: Oh my Gill, 'ow you suffer. She have been upon the rack, Zac.

ZAC: To satisfy my wife, Mak, say again, you would not steal from us.

MAK: I would rather eat my own child than steal from you, Zac.

ZAC: Aye — let me see the child.

[Gill groans.]

MIRIAM: Come away, Zac, I can find nothing.

ZAC: Lord, your lad smells ripe, Mak.

GILL: He's not well....

ZAC: An' Gill reeks too. I've never smelt a pair so loud.

MIRIAM: Come away, Zac.

MAK: I covered 'em in goose grease to keep the cold away.

MIRIAM: Zac.

ZAC: Mak, we 'ave been mistaken. May you, Gill and yer boy prosper and flourish.

MAK: Thankee, Zac.

ZAC: Don't take offence at the manner of our arriving.

MAK: Nor will I at the manner of yer going. Farewell.

[Miriam and Zac leave — Miriam is deep in thought. Behind them Mak and Gill prepare to slaughter the lamb.]

ZAC: Satisfied?

MIRIAM: Since we 'ave been mistaken I shall make amends. Give me a farthing, husband, I shall make a gift of it to the child as is custom.

[She gives the baby to Zac.]

[Mak raises the knife.]

MIRIAM: Mak —

[They put down the knife and Gill scrambles back into bed.]

I be back with a gift for the child.

[She enters.]

MAK: Miriam, Gill needs rest and the boy is fast asleep.

MIRIAM: My — I thought I saw him peep. Give me leave to kiss him, Mak.

[Gill groans.]

MAK: Can you not leave us be?

MIRIAM: Lift up the child and bring him out.

[They struggle.]

My — he have a long snout!

MAK: Aye, the poor boy is misshapen.

GILL: But we love him still for all his faults.

MIRIAM: For sure he be ill made, though I think he keeps the looks of Gill.

GILL: Get out — Get out I say!

[Zac has been watching — the three round the bed are struggling.]

ZAC: Miriam. *[they struggle]* Miriam!

[They stop.]

MIRIAM and GILL and MAK: What?

ZAC: That's a sheep. It's no boy. It's a sheep.

MIRIAM: No!

MAK: A sheep? How dare you call my son and heir a sheep —

[Miriam pulls the sheep out at last.]

MIRIAM: Lo Mak's heir.

GILL: Mercy, 'ave mercy on us.

MAK: Zac, listen — this be no sheep — it be our boy who were bewitched.

GILL: We will repay you — double and double again.

MIRIAM: Shut up.

ZAC: 'Twas me who were bewitched, Mak.

MAK: No, no, he were bewitched by an elf — as the clock struck twelve, our poor son were horribly misshapen — like a sheep. See.

[He wails and cries.]

ZAC: I know our sheep by its ear mark, Mak.

GILL: I told 'ee to cut off its ear mark, Mak. I throw myself on yer mercy, Zac.

[She grabs his legs.]

ZAC: Let go of my trousers....

GILL: We danced together, Zac, at the autumn sheep fair; you remember. Could you see me dance now on the end of a rope? I know you for a better man.

ZAC: Come away, Miriam, we shall leave.

MIRIAM: Leave? I shall go straight way to the magistrate and tell on them.

ZAC: I will not have their deaths upon me. Come, we have our sheep.

MIRIAM: *[she grabs the knife]* Then I shall punish them here and now, and be done.

ZAC: We be no judges, we be shepherds. Now come

away.

MIRIAM: This thief will pay.

GILL: Mercy. Mercy.

MAK: I am no thief. I gave ee cider and you gave me nothing in return. I gave you a toy for yer child and you gave me nothing in return — so I took the lamb in return.

MIRIAM: I shall have some justice done here before I leave.

ZAC: Then punish him as he deserves, with ridicule, an' toss him in a blanket.

[Silence.]

MIRIAM: Toss him in a blanket? These wretched folk steal the food from our mouths and you say toss 'im in a blanket?

ZAC: *[almost nose to nose with Miriam]* Aye, a blanket.

MAK: Aye. See we 'ave a blanket here in which to toss me.

ZAC: That's my blanket, Mak.

MAK: Ah! Then 'tis fitting 'tis the scene of my humiliation.

MIRIAM: *[in disbelief]* Hah — and how shall us two toss him?

[There then follows an improvised section of 'horse-play'. See notes on the original production at the front of the script.]

ZAC: There, 'tis done.

MIRIAM: What about 'er?

ZAC: Leave 'er be.

MIRIAM: Aye. I see it clear now. "Leave 'er be" ee says.

ZAC: 'Tis time to go.

MIRIAM: I see now what yer honesty and nobility have hid.

ZAC: You make no sense, Miriam, you be tired — come....

MIRIAM: Aye, let us quickly from this hovel — you knows it all too well I reckon, after "dancing".

ZAC: Miriam?

MIRIAM: Who is the man here when Mak is away so long in Bethlehem?

ZAC: You 'ave lost yer reason, Miriam, you are exhausted.

MIRIAM: You even let Mak steal from you, pretending to be some kind of fool... and how you resisted coming here to reclaim our property, and when 'tis done, you will do no more than "toss him in a blanket", and as for her — leave 'er be you say — 'tis all guilt — I see it now — guilt.

GILL: 'Ow dare ee say —

MIRIAM: Shut up! I shall reclaim all that is mine — my sheep, my blanket and my husband.

[Exit Miriam.]

[Exit Zac.]

[Silence. Mak stares at Gill.]

GILL: Mak? Mak, you're frightening me. Don't hit me.

MAK: Why should I hit you?

GILL: She is lying, Mak, a filthy lie. *[silence]* You'd take her word above mine? Mak? Mak?

[She approaches and he grabs her roughly.]

MAK: I found ee dancing alone in the corner of an ale house, yer head full of clouds an' incense an' lord knows what else. There were nothing left you but the brothel.

[Gill pulls away. He throws down her belongings.]

GILL: Mak? Mak? What is happening? I cannot understand. You said you loved me.

MAK: I lied. I be a liar an' a cheat. I said what I was, and you said you might be trusted. Until that time I 'ave never trusted to another soul nor shall I again.

GILL: You cannot stay here alone, Mak.

MAK: I was alone before....

GILL: Aye, and in a pit of misery. You need me.

MAK: Get out!

GILL: She 'ave lied. She lies I tell you.

MAK: *[shrugs]* Go, while yer face is still unmarked. I shall not say it more — Go!

GILL: Where shall I go?

MAK: I care not — an' if ee ever comes back, you shall not find me here.

SCENE SIX

[Miriam and Zac are walking back, Miriam with the baby, Zac with the lamb. Miriam chortles to herself.]

ZAC: 'Tis no laughing matter.

MIRIAM: *[she laughs]* You should 'ave seen Mak's face, darker than a thundercloud. Much like yer own face, sweet husband.

ZAC: You 'ave accused me, in public, of adultery.

[She laughs.]

With a girl 'alf my age.

MIRIAM: Serves ee right, you great lammick — for not giving the thieves the punishment they deserve. Serves ee right for letting that dirty fox make a fool out of ee. *[pause]* Toss him in a blanket indeed. Thought you to make a fool out of me an' all?

ZAC: I thought to show ee how ridiculous a judge you were. *[silence]* And how wrong it is to punish a man who steals out of hunger. You have brought me down. The word will spread across the hills that I, Zacariah Williams....

[She laughs.]

Will you cease laughing!

MIRIAM: You, 'usband, are a pompous piece o' foot rot! As if you've never glanced at a young girl at market.

ZAC: I 'ave not.

MIRIAM: I seed you looking. Aye, even at that good for nothing Gill.

ZAC: I 'ave not. I 'ave not. I 'ave not.

MIRIAM: Three times "I 'ave not".

[Miriam and Zac arrive back to find Gill by the fire. She is breathing hard. They stand open mouthed.]

GILL: I ran all the way.

MIRIAM: Go away. You hear me. Go away.

GILL: Go where? 'E 'ave thrown me out, 'cos of you an' yer vile lies.

MIRIAM: Don't just stand there with yer mouth gaping like a fly trap, get rid of her.

ZAC: Know you some spell that I may make her vanish in a puff of smoke?

MIRIAM: She is at our fire. That woman is 'ere.

ZAC: As you 'ave sown, so shall you reap.

[Miriam kicks him.]

ZAC: Will you not....

MIRIAM: You were took in by Mak, an' now you will be taken in by his accomplice. He 'ave sent 'er to steal again, knowing that the worst ee must face is yer ole blanket.

GILL: I 'ave come because I 'ave nowhere else to go. That's the truth of it.

ZAC: Oh, I know not. I care not. I am driven to my wits' end.

MIRIAM: A shortish journey, I do suppose.

GILL: I need some food.

MIRIAM: What you need is a thwack round the ear, my girl.

ZAC: If 'er 'usband 'ave thrown 'er out because of you, we must offer some compensation.

MIRIAM: Husband? You think they be married?

ZAC: Give the girl some bread.

MIRIAM: Never — I 'ave kept this bread so far an' no way will I let it go.

ZAC: Sit by the fire, Gill.

MIRIAM: Stand.

ZAC: Sit.

MIRIAM: Stand.

ZAC: Sit.

MIRIAM: Aye, go on then sit, my 'usband 'ave the goodwill of an angel and the brains of a frog. Sit.

ZAC: Why do you keep on so?

MIRIAM: Because nothing I say makes no difference to nothing. The man have the last say, "We shall pay our Poll Tax", "We shall let Mak stay", "We shall toss him in a blanket","She shall sit by the fire". I am never listened to.

[Gill bursts into tears.]

ZAC: Now, now, now.

MIRIAM: Get yer paws off her.

ZAC: Is there no end to yer cruelty?

MIRIAM: If she 'ave been thrown out by Mak she is lucky. Better off without him.

GILL: You don't know him.

MIRIAM: Oh I knows him.

GILL: He's a good man at heart.

MIRIAM: Just had a hard life I suppose.

GILL: Yes!

MIRIAM: Haven't we all, but we don't end like Mak. The man has no more heart than an axe. Why would you be here else?

GILL: Because of you.

MIRIAM: *[she considers]* If I owe ee anything it's to put you straight. Mak have taken you in. He's had other girls to help him pick pockets at market, but when they starts demanding things of him they are out, as you are out. He changes his face an' his voice to suit the person he is about to rob, an' ee 'ave robbed you. He is no good.

[Silence.]

ZAC: You come with us tomorrow, to Bethlehem, and we'll find you work, I'm sure of it.

MIRIAM: I'll count the flock.

ZAC: Aye.

[She leaves Zac with the baby. Zac gives the baby to Gill while he stokes the fire.]

GILL: What is the child's name?

ZAC: We are in some disagreement about his name. *[pause]* Would you like to have a child, Gill?

GILL: Why, Zac, I hardly knows ee.

ZAC: Why does everyone want to make a fool o' me?

GILL: I'm sorry, it was a joke.

[Miriam re-enters and takes the baby.]

MIRIAM: Are you mad? She is like to run off and sell the child at market.

ZAC: I must sleep.

MIRIAM: Aye go on, sleep. You'll be better company.

[Zac sighs.]

ZAC: Let us hope we have come to the end of this night's interruptions. Goodnight.

MIRIAM: *[to Gill]* I'm watching you.

[Miriam starts to sing the lullaby to the baby. Gill joins in, momentarily Miriam stops.]

[The lullaby sounds Jewish, and is used later in the scene between Mary and Miriam.]

SCENE SEVEN

[Miriam, Zac and Gill sleep. Miriam falls to sleep immediately. Gill is left. Suddenly there is a strange light and beautiful music. Gill walks to the side of the camp and looks out into the darkness.]

GILL: Zac. Zac.

ZAC: *[wakes with a start]* What?

GILL: Something's going on.

ZAC: Hey.

GILL: Listen.

[Silence.]

It's fading now.

ZAC: What is?

GILL: The music. Did you not hear it?

ZAC: I... well... no... I... well I might have. What kind of music?

GILL: Can't rightly say.

ZAC: Probably them three shepherds over yonder 'aving a knees up, as they are like to do.

GILL: The shepherds?

[She runs to the edge of the camp.]

They have gone now. They were there, and they were bathed in this incredible light — and now they've gone.

[Miriam wakes.]

MIRIAM: What's going on?

[Zac takes a step away from Gill to illustrate their separateness.]

What are you two up to?

ZAC: Nothing.

MIRIAM: Why are you standing over there then?

ZAC: She heard some music — saw some lights.

MIRIAM: Oh Aye — Music? Lights?

GILL: Music like you've never heard before. Lights like... like... I 'ave no words for 'em.

[Miriam is taken by her seriousness.]

MIRIAM: 'Twas a dream no doubt.

GILL: I was awake — as I am now. I swear it.

MIRIAM: It be hunger an' the thin air of these hills, it do often make us see things, 'tis well known. Take no note of it an' go to sleep, both of ee.

[Miriam falls to sleep.]

GILL: Zac. You believe me.

ZAC: Aye. It's in my nature to believe. Long nights have I stared at the stars, an' on some nights — it's like I can get myself out of my skin, and float away into the bigness of things, and from out there I look back an' see what fools we be to spend our lives in small and hurtful squabbles. Then I come back, and I tell no-one of my journey 'cos they would not believe me.

GILL: But do you go — do ee really go — and leave the world behind?

ZAC: It don't matter what is real or not. It matters only what it means.

GILL: What does this music mean then, and these lights?

MIRIAM: Will you stop blabbering and go to sleep.

ZAC: That's for you to say.

GILL: But what about the Angel?

ZAC: What Angel?

[Enter the oriental king.]

SCENE EIGHT

[The king stumbles into the camp calling for help. He is blindfolded and his hands are tied behind his back. Miriam jumps up from her sleep with a scream and the three back away.]

KING: Help me. Help me. I have been robbed. *[silence]* Please. I know there's someone there. I heard voices and ran towards them. *[silence]* I did not mean to startle you. Are you still there? Will you not help me! *[silence]* I have nothing else — I cannot be robbed. You see my robes, I am a king. If any harm comes to me, Herod's soldiers will punish you. *[pause]* They are not far behind me.

[Zac moves forward and takes off his blindfold.]

Am I safe?

ZAC: Aye — you're safe.

KING: Who are you?

ZAC: I be a shepherd — and you?

KING: I am a King.

[Miriam kneels and urges Gill to do the same. Zac unties his hands.]

I thought they would kill me. *[to women]* Please, come forward.

[The women do not move.]

[He commands] Come forward!

[They step forward.]

Your wife and daughter?

ZAC: My wife and... and....

KING: There is no need to explain....

ZAC: No, she is....

KING: *[he raises his hand to silence Zac]* You have a child? *[Zac nods]* A boy?

ZAC: Aye.

KING: Show me the boy. Give me the boy. *[silence]* I would see the boy — Please. I will do him no harm. On my word.

ZAC: I am not so trusting of people's words as I once was.

KING: Please.

[Zac nods at Miriam. The King takes the boy.]

KING: What is his name?

ZAC: We be undecided — disagreement. You be a long way from home.

KING: Yes, I am searching for someone, *[he gives the baby back]* but I have not found him yet. My friends and I were following a star that appeared in the East, I have lost sight of it now.

ZAC: Where be yer friends to?

KING: They left me behind when my camel became lame, it was then I was robbed. The star was there — is there a town in that direction?

ZAC: Aye, Bethlehem.

KING: Bethlehem. Perhaps in the morning you would show me the way to Bethlehem.

ZAC: Aye — but if I were you, I wouldn't start from here.

KING: Where would be the best place then?

ZAC: Down on the road sir — where the sign says to Bethlehem — in nice bold letters.

KING: *[laughs]* I am among good honest 'simple' folk.

[Silence. Miriam brings forth the bread.]

ZAC: *[whispers to Miriam]* What are you thinking of? That is all we have — you have spent the night....

[She pushes through him.]

KING: Thank you.

[He eats.]

I must sleep now.

[Miriam takes the blanket off Zac's shoulders. They have

a short fight over it, which Zac loses when she kicks him in the shins again. Miriam lays the blanket down.]

ZAC: Aye sleep. Be our guest. 'Tis Guest-night!

KING: By the time I count to seven I shall be asleep. Do not be alarmed, it is an ancient trick of the East. Watch over me gentle shepherds. 1... 2... 3... 4... 5... 6... 7.

[Zac, Miriam and Gill fall instantly to sleep.]

KING: *[in bad temper]* No. No. No. I fall asleep. I... I... I... I. 7... 6... 5... 4... 3... 2... 1.

[He falls asleep.]

ZAC: *[imitates]* I... I... I... I.

[Gill creeps up and touches his robe.]

MIRIAM: Keep away from him. Have you no respect?

GILL: Did you see the weight inside his robe? He have something yet which the robbers did not find.

[There is a moment of glances between them.]

MIRIAM: Zac?

[Short reprise of song 'You Shall Not Steal'. Zac takes the myrrh. Miriam is open mouthed.]

SONG: You shall not
You shall not
No, you shall not
You shall not steal

ZAC: Come wife — don't stand there with yer mouth gaping like a fly trap. We must go to Bethlehem!

END OF ACT ONE.

Act Two

SCENE ONE

[Gill, Miriam and Zac are walking towards Bethlehem.]

MIRIAM: Slow down, Zac, slow down.

ZAC: Us must get as far from the scene of the crime as we possibly can.

MIRIAM: Whatever was ee thinking on? Us'll 'ave soldiers now chasin' all over looking for us.

ZAC: Well hurry then.

MIRIAM: I am hurrying. I am no hare.

[Zac stops. Miriam walks into him.]

GILL: Why are you stopping?

ZAC: Miriam said....

MIRIAM: I said slow down — not stop.

ZAC: I'll carry the baby for a distance.

MIRIAM: Aye, but be careful.

ZAC: This babe'll never be in safer hands.

[They walk.]

MIRIAM: A king? Of all the men to rob, you had to go and rob a king.

GILL: And what did ee rob from him I'd like to know?

ZAC: We must press on.

GILL: Could be anything. Could be silver.

MIRIAM: For a man oo never stoled a thing in his life, you chose a fine victim. A king. A king! I can't get over it.

ZAC: Ee were no king in my eyes.

MIRIAM: Hey?

ZAC: Ee took the blanket off me back, an' the bread from me belly. A king!

MIRIAM: Mind the baby.

ZAC: A king don't steal from his own subjects.

MIRIAM: Course ee does — it's called taxes.

ZAC: That's different.

MIRIAM: You have a cockeyed view of the world, Zacariah Williams. In fact you 'ave no view of the world at all, yer 'ed is wrapped in a fog. That is my confirmed opinion.

GILL: It could be gold. Surely we can look now?

ZAC: I have no care what it is. I didn't take it for what it is. I took it on principle.

MIRIAM: Here they come, his principles, to pester us like summer midges.

GILL: Surely we can see what we 'ave. 'Tis foolish to do otherwise.

MIRIAM: We are not common thieves. Still, perhaps we should 'ave a look. Zac. Zac.

[Zac gives Miriam the baby, and puts the package down and carefully unwraps it.]

MIRIAM: What's that there?

ZAC: Some sort of dust — smells like incense.

GILL: That's myrrh that is.

ZAC: Myrrh?

MIRIAM: Myrrh. *[she nods]* Myrrh. Well done 'usband, ee 'ave stolen the least useful substance known to common folk. We can't eat it, we can't wear it. If ee'd stolen his socks, 'twould 'ave been of more benefit an' as much incense. Give it here, I'll throw it in the hedge.

GILL: No. 'Tis worth summat. We'll find the right man in Bethlehem to sell it to, if we ask around. I knows the places. Mak says everything is of value to someone.

MIRIAM: I told ee to forget Mak. Us'll 'ave no dealings in Mak's world.

GILL: It's worth something to someone, I knows it.

MIRIAM: Then I shall keep it.

ZAC: Keep it, I care not.

MIRIAM: Where are you going to?

ZAC: I sense a short cut.

MIRIAM: What short cut? I see no short cut.

ZAC: I be a man of the hills, I 'ave a nose fer such things.

MIRIAM: I puts no more trust in yer nose than in any other part of ee.

ZAC: I have ancient instincts.

MIRIAM: An' I 'ave a child. We must stick to the path — it's a perfectly suitable path.

ZAC: We'll save an hour's walk, an' arrive afore dark.

MIRIAM: What if us gets lost?

ZAC: I knows these hills better than I knows my own mind — an' I'll thank ee not to comment on that.

GILL: Short cut sounds good to me.

[She joins Zac.]

MIRIAM: You shall know some rough weather, Zacariah Williams, if this do go wrong.

ZAC: This way.

[They walk, Zac leading.]

GILL: Can we stop?

ZAC: Yes.

MIRIAM: No.

GILL: I've got a stone in my boot.

MIRIAM: What?

ZAC: She has a stone....

MIRIAM: I heard. Us must get to Bethlehem afore the curfew.

ZAC: We be about 'alf way, I reckon. We may as well stop to rest.

GILL: Pull the boot off, Zac.

[He pulls the boot off.]

MIRIAM: Hurry up — the baby likes to keep moving.

ZAC: Yer foot is all bloody — why didn't ee say?

GILL: Didn't want to slow us down. What's that?

ZAC: I use it on the sheep. Won't do ee any harm.

[Zac massages horse liniment into her foot.]

GILL: Hey that's lovely that is.

MIRIAM: It's only her big toe, not 'er whole leg.

ZAC: As in life, Miriam, all things be connected.

MIRIAM: Bah! Load of ol' droppings that is!

ZAC: *[as he rubs her leg]* Bethlehem. Aye. Us'll be King an' Queen tonight, Miriam. A tidy inn, a proper meal, an' some cheerful company.

MIRIAM: Us won't be together then?

ZAC: *[ignores her]* Maybe us'll 'ave a dance like we used to.

[He dances and Gill laughs.]

MIRIAM: What are you laughing at?

GILL: His dancing.

MIRIAM: "Our" dancing is no laughing matter.

[Zac stops. Gill gets up.]

GILL: I saw some berries in the woods.

MIRIAM: You stay 'ere!

GILL: Mak says it's always worth 'avin' summat to bargain with in a city.

[Exit Gill.]

ZAC: Why so sharp with 'er? She means no 'arm.

MIRIAM: I am not blind.

ZAC: I don't recall accusin' ee of being blind!

MIRIAM: Her "toe", her "leg".

ZAC: Oh, Miriam.

MIRIAM: There ee goes with his "Oh, Miriam". Always telling me what I see with my own eyes isn't true. 'Tis a wonder I have kept my sanity.

ZAC: There's another thing I never accused ee of. *[silence]* Why do you drive me to make such cold remarks? They are not worthy of me.

[Gill comes in with some berries.]

GILL: Look.

[She holds them out. She reads the atmosphere between them and lowers her hands.]

MIRIAM: Come on then. If yer coming.

[They walk. Zac stops.]

What?

[Zac looks around.]

We're lost id'n we?

ZAC: No....

MIRIAM: It were a perfectly good path. I was fond of that path.

ZAC: We are not lost.

MIRIAM: But you had to follow yer nose.

ZAC: We are not lost.

MIRIAM: Where are we then?

ZAC: Why do folk 'ave to know where they are all the time? 'Tis the curse of modern times. I'll tell ee where you are, you are 'ere. Zacariah Williams is never lost!

MIRIAM: *[to Gill]* This is what I 'ave to put up with.

GILL: Don't talk to me about it. I likes him well enough.

[Miriam stares at her.]

ZAC: The choice is this, us either goes through the brambles — there; or us goes through the bog — there.

GILL: There's no route through them brambles....

ZAC: Through the bog then.

MIRIAM: We can go back — to the path.

ZAC: I will not go back.

MIRIAM: We have a baby.

ZAC: It's not dangerous. *[he jumps across]* See. Come, Miriam.

GILL: Give me.

[Miriam gives her the baby.]

MIRIAM: If I die, I shall never forgive ee.

[She comes across.]

ZAC: Right....

MIRIAM: She's not coming over with my baby. Go back!

[Zac goes back. Gill then goes over leaving Zac with the baby.]

MIRIAM: Stop there... there... there. Zac. Zac. Where are you going? Zac.

ZAC: I am sinking, Miriam. All those things I said I....

MIRIAM: The baby, Zac — the baby....

ZAC: Don't panic, Miriam — Don't panic.

[Zac either throws baby or passes baby along audience.]

The crook. The crook.

[Zac falls in the mire. They pull him out. Gill laughs.]

Go on, laugh. It'll do you good.

MIRIAM: *[to Gill]* Oh very funny. 'Twouldna be so funny if ee were dead.

GILL: Ee was never near dead. *[she laughs]*

MIRIAM: I weren't talking about him. What care I if ee sinks in a bog? He can take his nose and ancient instincts down with him. Short cut — I'll give ee short cut.

GILL: Look. Look. Bethlehem. You 'ave found the way, Zac. You 'ave found the way.

ZAC: Aye, indeed I have.

[Miriam kicks him.]

MIRIAM: I hate you!

SCENE TWO

[Bethlehem]

SONG: Oh little town of Bethlehem
How still we see thee lie.
Above thy deep and dreamless sleep,
The silent stars go by.
Yet in thy dark streets shineth
The everlasting light.
The hopes and fears of all the years
Are met in thee tonight.

ZAC: Well, here us be.

MIRIAM: How shall we ever find our way?

GILL: I will take ee.

ZAC: Excuse me, my Good Man, we 'ave come to pay our taxes. Where do us register an' all? Oh tomorrow. I thankee. I asks where, an' ee answers when. That's how the city answers ee, all front to back.

GILL: Keep close together.

MIRIAM: There's a strong smell of something.

ZAC: That, Miriam, is humanity. An' I 'ave just trod in a sizeable lump of it.

GILL: The best inns an' taverns are all on t'other side of the market, down one road. We'll have to push our way through.

MIRIAM: Zac! Zac!

ZAC: I will give this poor beggar a sixpence.

MIRIAM: You will not.

ZAC: Miriam, he is poor, hungry and homeless.

[Miriam regards the audience.]

MIRIAM: Aye, an' so is that one, and that one, an' that one.

Shall ee give sixpence to every one, and how shall ee choose which is the most deserving?

ZAC: His eyes implore me — so red-rimmed.

MIRIAM: Aye, full of cider, which be all yer sixpence will buy. 'Twill do no good, now come away.

ZAC: No good? How can an act of goodness be thus described?

GILL: Zac, put yer money down lest you be robbed.

ZAC: Robbed?

GILL: Aye, an' with violence.

ZAC: Keep the child close to ee, Miriam. We are in Hell's Kitchen.

GILL: This way.

ZAC: Here. I seed some red lights down that small street, which look welcoming enough — and a young woman beckoning....

MIRIAM: Just follow Gill, you daft old infant!

ZAC: Aye, we be right glad to 'ave you 'ere, Gill, for I am truly lost now, in the very place I sought to find.

GILL: Soldiers!

[The soldiers approach. Music.]

ZAC: Aye, Sir, aye from the country. My wife, my son and....

GILL: Daughter.

ZAC: Aye, daughter — we be all one family, Sir. Aye, we will. God save the King. *[they go]* Give a farm boy a sword an' ee thinks ee rules the world.

[Music fades.]

GILL and MIRIAM: Sssh!

ZAC: 'Tisn't right. 'Tis all front to back.

MIRIAM: Zac — see there on t'other side.

ZAC: What?

MIRIAM: The three shepherds from over yonder hill.

GILL: Keep close or your will lose each other within yards.

ZAC: Hey — Hey! 'Tis we. Zac and Miriam. How be ee sheps? What? Can't hear. Who? Son of who? Speak up man.

[They go.]

MIRIAM: What did they say?

ZAC: Couldn't catch it — but they had smiles on their faces wider than the gaps between their ears. I'd say there was a drop o' drink behind those grins.

GILL: Come on. The first curfew will be sounding soon — if we are found outside we shall be locked up.

ZAC: They cannot lock up the whole world.

GILL: Try this place.

ZAC: "The Old Boar's Inn."

MIRIAM: Ee shall be if we stay 'ere.

[Knock.}

ZAC: Good evening, Sir. My wife and I, and my son and....

GILL: Daughter.

MIRIAM: Get on with it.

ZAC: Be seeking a room for one night. No. No. Very well. I thank ee, we shall try further down. *[door slams]*

[They move down.]

ZAC: 'Ere's one. "The Nag's Rest". *[pause]* Do ee want to stay 'ere, Miriam?

[She kicks him.]

MIRIAM: Just find us a room, an' hurry.

[He knocks.]

ZAC: Good evening, Sir — Madam — Sir — Forgive me, these city styles do confuse a country man.

[Door slams.]

I think that means he or she has no vacancies.

[They move down.]

ZAC: "The No Room At The Inn Inn".

[Knock. The door opens. He looks in and then down.]

Ah. Is yer mother or father in? No. Well... Oh you are no child. Forgive me. I meant no rudeness. We are looking for somewhere to put our heads down for the night. You 'ave? How much? — 40 shekels?

MIRIAM: Haggle. Haggle.

ZAC: With my wife — 60.

MIRIAM: Haggle. Haggle.

ZAC: With my daughter — 70.

MIRIAM: Haggle. Haggle.

ZAC: But the baby must come in free.

[The door is slammed.]

MIRIAM: I told you to haggle.

ZAC: I be among the best hagglers of Old Radnor, but I be out of my depth when haggling with a child — he has an unfair advantage.

MIRIAM: You be the only person I ever heard haggle the price up.

ZAC: We'll try this one over 'ere.

MIRIAM: Slow down.

ZAC: Follow the crook — above the crowd.

MIRIAM: Zac. Zac. Where are you, Zac?

ZAC: Here.

MIRIAM: Where?

GILL: Zac. Miriam.

ZAC: Can you see the crook? Miriam. Miriam.

GILL and MIRIAM: Zac!

ZAC: My crook — follow the crook!

[She turns round.]

MIRIAM: Zac... Zac... Zac...

GILL: Zac... Zac...

SCENE THREE

ZAC: Gill. Gill. Where's Miriam to?

GILL: She were over there but a moment ago, but I cannot see 'er now. Miriam. Miriam.

ZAC: Miriam.

[Silence.]

Infernal city — I knowed it would be like this. She is lost, and the curfew is not long to go.

GILL: Don't worry so.

ZAC: She will never find 'er way through the maze of streets. She could be murdered, stole, sold into slavery. An' the baby. Oh what have I done? Miriam. Miriam.

GILL: Zac. Zac. 'Tis alright — if it comes to the worst she will meet us at the place of registration tomorrow.

ZAC: Aye. Aye. I do hate the city, Gill. The country brings out what's of value in a person, but the city hides all manner of folk. Nothing is what it seems, you cannot tell the good from the bad, even the children are not children. Oh Miriam. Miriam.

GILL: 'Tis a wonder to me you should fret so. She would not do the same for you.

ZAC: Miriam is not so 'ard at 'art as ee might suppose.

GILL: Why does she kick you then? Like an unwanted dog.

ZAC: 'Tis but a sign of affection, Gill, that 'ave been twisted by the hardness of our life.

GILL: She says she hates the very sight of you.

ZAC: By hate, she means love. Most things have two meanings, you'll learn that as ee gets older. Us'll stop here for a while an' see if she finds 'er way back.

[Gill takes out the berries she picked, and offers some to Zac.]

ZAC: You picked 'em, you eat them.

GILL: Go on.

ZAC: Thank ee. *[he eats]* No sign of Mak then?

GILL: No!

ZAC: I thought p'rhaps ee went into that betting shop to see if ee was there.

GILL: What if I did? It's no business o' yours.

[She takes the berries from him.]

ZAC: Miriam is right in one thing. Mak is best left alone.

GILL: Mak is not so 'ard at 'art as ee might suppose.

ZAC: Aye.

GILL: I must find him. I must put things back. It will be the same between us again. I know him.

ZAC: I be mighty sorry she 'ave put ee in this misery with 'er vile slander. Where those words came from, I don't know. She do 'ave such hate in 'er. I do nothing but try to make life pleasant, a short cut here, a short cut there, but no thanks do I get.

[Pause.]

I tries to give life a little meaning, an' she curses me for it. She sees nothing in life but the next moment — I 'ave never seed 'er look up at the stars, not once. "What use is they," she says, "to man or beast, 'anging there out of reach?" When us was courting, I would say "Look at the moon, see its light along the water." And she would say "I 'ave ten guineas, three sheep and a Welsh dresser, so now's the time to marry." So us married.

[Silence.]

An' what 'ave she become? All skin an' grief, that's Miriam. She reckons that this 'ere life is the full basket of eggs, an' I knows it's not. I just knows it. She is cursed with reality. And so us knocks along, spitting an' scratching, an' I do hate her so for bringing me so base in thought. She have no right to make me 'ate her so. No right.

GILL: Why don't you leave her then?

ZAC: Aye. I should an' all. She 'ave accused you an' I of the unthinkable — as if you an' I. I am twice yer age.

GILL: At least.

ZAC: 'Tis the 'ard weather than roughens the skin. I am not so old as I seem — though I've lost a few teeth.

[Gill laughs. Miriam enters and watches from a dis-

tance.]

GILL: Oh, Zac, you could find another woman. You be kind and good, as a man should be.

ZAC: An' you be the same, Gill. Kind and good. I can see it in you.

GILL: I can't be called good. You don't know the 'alf of what I've done.

ZAC: I knows what I see.

GILL: I've stolen from people worse off than me.

ZAC: You were driven to it.

GILL: I've slept with men for money.

ZAC: You 'ad no choice, I don't suppose.

GILL: I lied before the law, an' I've seen terrible things....

ZAC: Aye, but ee 'ave seen an angel an' all — and ee must not forget it.

GILL: It were no angel. Just a trick of light I reckon.

ZAC: Maybe it was yer own reflection then.

[Gill touches Zac's cheek, and on an impulse they embrace. Song: 'You Shall Not Commit Adultery'.]

SONG: You shall not
No, you shall not
No, you shall not
No, you shall not commit adultery
No, no, no, so says the holy Bible

You shall not, no, no, no, you shall not
No, you shall not, no, no, no, you shall not
You shall not commit adultery
No, no, no, so says the holy Bible

Can you carry fire in your heart and not burn
your clothes? — I'm asking you

Can you walk upon hot coals and your feet not get scorched?
Can you carry fire in your heart and not burn your clothes? — I'm asking you
Can you walk upon hot coals and your feet not get scorched?

Rather, rejoice, rejoice, rejoice, rejoice
Rejoice, rejoice — In the love of your youth (x4)

ZAC: Ah... ow... ow...!

GILL: What is it?

ZAC: Cramp. I got terrible cramp.

[The curfew bell rings.]

GILL: Curfew. Quickly, we must hide.

[Exit.]

SCENE FOUR

[Miriam wanders the streets alone.]

INKEEPER: Yes...Yes...Yes wife. I'll lock the doors.

MIRIAM: Hello. Hello.

[The inkeeper enters with a mop.]

MIRIAM: I'm looking for a room.

INKEEPER: *[refers to the mop]* Washin' up, stacks of it. *[he hears his wife]* Excuse me. *[to his wife]* Yes, yes, I'll be with ee in a moment, there's someone at the door see. Yes... yes, I'll tell 'em.

MIRIAM: Oh, you 'ave no rooms then.

INKEEPER: Yes, we 'ave no rooms.

MIRIAM: I don't mind sharing.

INKEEPER: It's the busiest night I can remember. All the rooms are being shared. Folk sleeping 'ed to toe.

MIRIAM: I see. Thank ee.

[She turns to go.]

INKEEPER: *[to his wife offstage]* Yes, yes, give the guests what we have. *[to Miriam]* Wait a moment, we be under some pressure.

MIRIAM: I don't mind where I sleep, I just want to get off the street.

INKEEPER: We do 'ave a stable at the back of the inn.

MIRIAM: That's fine. 'Ow much?

INKEEPER: You will 'ave to share.

MIRIAM: I don't care. 'Ow much?

INKEEPER: There be two adults an' a baby.

MIRIAM: Just tell me 'ow much.

INKEEPER: An' there be animals an' all. An' no bed to sleep on, only straw.

MIRIAM: Will you not answer me, man? 'Ow much shall I pay ee fer the stable?

[Silence. He shakes his head, and makes her put away the money.]

INKEEPER: *[to his wife]* Yes, yes, I'll be there now, in a minute — *[to Miriam]* Pressure see. Please this way. The woman you be sharin' with 'ad 'er baby yesterday. She 'ad no cot, so us put 'er in the manger. Hah. Fancy that.

[They walk past the audience, and the inkeeper chats to them as if they were guests. While he does this, Mary and Joseph enter and prepare themselves for the nativity scene. There is music, again of a heavenly nature, and the image is one from a painting, idealised. As the music finishes, Joseph sleeps and Mary comforts the baby Jesus.]

SCENE FIVE

[The stable. Enter Inkeeper and Miriam.]

INKEEPER: 'Ere us be then. This is Mrs from um...uh...and this Mr and Mrs from um...well come over to the kitchen in the morning. Breakfast is 'tween seven an' nine. No latecomers, 'cept those who don't make it by nine.

MIRIAM: Thankee.

INKEEPER: *[calls]* Yes, dear wife, I'm coming now. *[to Miriam]* Such pressure. Goodnight.

[He exits.]

MIRIAM: I'll sit down 'ere is it?

MARY: Aye.

MIRIAM: Smells ripe in 'ere.

MARY: 'Tis all the livestock. Keeps the place warm though.

MIRIAM: Innkeeper said you give birth to that boy in 'ere.

MARY: Aye. Yesterday.

MIRIAM: You're alright then?

MARY: I were lucky. That's me 'usband — Joseph. Ee's right tuckered out.

MIRIAM: Well ee would be. Poor ol' boy's just 'ad a baby.

[They exchange smiles over this.]

MARY: Ee was born in Bethlehem see, so we 'ad to come 'ere to pay the tax.

MIRIAM: "Tax." Don't talk to me of no tax. Will King 'Erod pay such a tax? 'Eck as like. 'Tis one law for the rich and one for the poor. That's my confirmed opinion.

MARY: That's true enough.

MIRIAM: Aye, I said to my 'usband, we shouldn't pay that tax, but ee's a law abiding idiot!

MARY: Will ee be stopping 'ere an' all?

MIRIAM: No. A boy is it? Same as this one.

MARY: Aye.

MIRIAM: 'Tis a boy's world, so 'tis just as well. World is'n fit for woman when us 'as to give birth in stables an' open fields in rough weather.

MARY: What's yer boy called?

MIRIAM: Us 'ave been in disagreement over the boy's name. *[pause]* Amongst other things. I wants to call 'im Moses like the boy in the old book. Zac wants to call 'im Jesus. "Jesus", I says, "Why 'tis as common a name in these parts as 'Jones'". So ee's eight weeks old an' still no name. What's yers called?

MARY: *[pause]* Jesus.

MIRIAM: *[pause]* Aye. There you are see. The name is over common. *[pause]* Though 'tis nice enough.

[Curfew bell.]

MARY: There's the second curfew, all must be inside now. I 'ope yer 'usband 'ave found a bed for the night.

MIRIAM: I reckon ee 'ave. Sheets an' all. King an' Queen.

[She spits.]

[They rock the babies and sing the lullaby.]

Baby's dropped off, but I'm too tired to sleep.

MARY: Aye. We walked all the way from Nazareth.

MIRIAM: 'Twas nothing. We walked from t'other side of 'Ereford.

[Joseph turns in his sleep. Mary looks concerned.]

What's the matter?

MARY: I'm shaking — see.

MIRIAM: Got a fever?

MARY: No — I don't like this place of a sudden. The city, I mean.

MIRIAM: You alright?

MARY: Yes.

MIRIAM: Look like someone walked over yer grave.

[Pause.]

MARY: Please, keep talking to me. It'll keep my mind from worry.

MIRIAM: Worry of what?

MARY: I know not. Tell me of yer 'usband.

MIRIAM: Zac?

MARY: Aye.

MIRIAM: Him of the ancient instincts, the man of the stars, I could talk about him till Doomsday an' it wouldn't cheer ee up none.

MARY: A man of the stars?

MIRIAM: Aye. Ee sits up on the hill on a frostbitten night an' stares at 'em till ee goes crosseyed. Ee's so busy looking up ee don't see the army of thieves walking off with sheep under their arms. So it comes to me to save us from being fleeced at every turn. I should 'ave seed it comin' when us were courtin'. I says to him, "I 'ave ten guineas, three sheep an' a Welsh dresser" — no mean dowry for a poor woman — an' you know what ee says? Ee just looks up after a time an' says, "Looks more like a saucepan than a plough".

[Silence.]

Bah! I should 'ave knowed then ee 'ad no eye for the future, 'cept in the way of 'destiny'. He thinks the world of destiny. I says to un, Zac, life is no destiny, for poor folk life is a lottery, a roll o' dice. I mean, if you an' I were to swap the babes in our arms 'ere an' now, who would ever be the wiser? *[pause]* No-one, that is my confirmed opinion.

But Zac didn't see it that way, ee always reckons we be on the road to somewhere else an' ee leaves the worry of the moment to me. An' I bend beneath the burden of it, an' then ee curses me for worrying. I can't say the rain is wet, or the wind is cold, for in Zac's eyes tid'n noble to cómplain. Instead you 'ave to stick yer 'ed in the stars an' forget about the world. You 'ave to sit an' wait for the meek to possess the land, an' delight ourselves in abundance. An' to pass the time you 'ave to find meaning an' honour in humble things. I can't pour a cup of tea near Zac without it 'aving universal significance.

I spawse you reckon there must be some good in this man. Well ee reckons so — thinks ee is goodness itself. Ee 'as principles. An' each principle casts us further down the ladder o' luck. Ee got us thrown out of our cottage on a principle. Aye, over the cruel killing of our sheep. How Zac loves his sheep. "Oh," ee says, "us'll take a few sheep an' roam the hills like they did in the days of Noah." Ee cares more for his sheep than ee do for me, an' our baby, an' I can't forgive him that.

[Pause.]

Whatever else ee do this night, I can't forgive that.

MARY: Look.

MIRIAM: What's that then?

MARY: Gold.

MIRIAM: Get away with ee.

MARY: 'Tis gold.

MIRIAM: Gold?

MARY: Aye. It were a gift from a King. Please take a few coins. We 'ave no need for it all.

MIRIAM: Gold?

[Mary nods.]

You can't go giving away gold.

MARY: Please take some.

MIRIAM: Well I... but you... this is... Bah, get away with ee. Tid'n gold.

MARY: It is.

[She offers it.]

MIRIAM: Why should ee give it to me? *[pause]* I couldn't take it for nothing. I don't want no charity. Ere.

[She gives the myrrh.]

MARY: What's this?

MIRIAM: Myrrh. *[Mary looks at her]* It were a gift from a King.

MARY: Ah!

MIRIAM: Ah!

[They make the exchange.]

However will I explain it to Zac?

[Joseph stirs in his sleep. Killing music, which is his dream, but when he wakes it does not fade.]

MARY: Joseph? Joseph?

[The music gets louder.]

Joseph? What is it? Joseph?

[Joseph wakes.]

MIRIAM: What's going on?

JOSEPH: Mary, we must go. The baby is in danger of his life.

[He sees Miriam.]

MARY: She's a friend.

JOSEPH: Be quick, wife, we must run, now.

MIRIAM: Where are you going?

JOSEPH: Take my advice, woman, leave this city, or hide yer baby so that no-one may find it.

MIRIAM: Why?

JOSEPH: There is no time. Do as I say.

MARY: Goodbye.

[They go.]

[The killing music now reaches a climax. Under the pressure of it Miriam retreats with her baby, taking up the same position that Mary had at the beginning of the scene, so that one recognizes the mirror image. The killing music stops.]

SONG: *['Thou Shalt Not Kill'.]*

You shall not kill (x4)
Whoever strikes a man so he dies
Shall be put to death (x3)
Whoever strikes a man so he dies
Shall be put to death (x3)
You shall not

[The killing music returns, in quieter form, as Mak, now a soldier, disguised by his helmet/mask, enters holding a knife.

While the music remains, the action remains on a symbolic level. Mak looks for the child, and when he is near it there is a desperate scramble, but Mak finds it and holds the knife above it, so there is a picture of a soldier holding a knife over a baby with a woman on her knees before him. The music stops.]

MIRIAM: Please, my baby — my baby. 'Ere — I have gold. I

will give ee gold — see.

[She holds out the gold and Mak takes it. He is about to give the child back when Zac and Gill enter.]

ZAC: Miriam!

[Mak again raises the knife.]

MIRIAM: No! No! No!

[Zac falls to his knees.]

ZAC: I beg you. I beg you.

[Gill walks forward. Mak retreats.]

GILL: Mak. Mak?

[He lowers the knife. Miriam rushes forward and takes the baby. Zac embraces her.]

GILL: Mak?

MAK: I knew not oo it were. I knew not it were them. I swears it.

[Gill takes the knife and then points it at Mak.]

ZAC: Gill!

[She stops, but there is still a moment of uncertainty.]

GILL: Mak?

MAK: Ee offered us 'alf his kingdom. All the wealth of the world. Don't look at me. Don't look at me.

[He slumps to his knees.]

ZAC: Come, Gill, come, wife, we must leave the city.

MIRIAM: What 'ave happened?

ZAC: Herod 'ave ordered the slaying of all boys under two years old. No-one knows why. Be quick, wife, we must run, now. Gill — Gill.

[They exit.]

[Miriam and Gill then turn, and addressing Mak who sits numbed centre stage, they sing 'The Song Of Ramah.']

SONG: A voice was heard in Ramah
Wailing and loud lamentation,
Rachel weeping for her children;
She refused to be consoled
Because they were no more.

[Exit.]

SCENE SIX

[Gill, Zac and Miriam are walking back to the camp. Gill walks ahead — morose, silent. Zac carries the baby. Gill stops.]

GILL: I shall leave ee 'ere an' go down this path.

ZAC: The path to the camp is this way.

GILL: Your camp.

ZAC: Aye, and you may share it with we for a time. We 'ave discussed it.

GILL: Share what? A fire? I can build a fire.

ZAC: Where do this path lead to?

[She shrugs.]

MIRIAM: Come back with us. It'll do ee no good to be out of company.

GILL: I shall find company enough.

[Pause.]

ZAC: Gill, you must put Mak from yer mind.

GILL: How may I put him from my mind? I should 'ave killed him, they should all be killed oo do such things against nature.

ZAC: I know not the rights and wrongs of that. 'Cept what the Old Book says.

MIRIAM: What shall us ever do then? Nothing?

GILL: How did ee come to such a thing, Mak? How did ee ever come to it, Mak?

[She is overcome and Miriam embraces her.]

MIRIAM: You should come back, for a few days at least.

GILL: No.

ZAC: You 'ave no money.

GILL: Neither 'ave you.

ZAC: You 'ave no shelter.

GILL: Neither 'ave you.

MIRIAM: Now she 'ave spoke true.

ZAC: But what will you do?

GILL: I will go down this path and see where it leads. What else may I do? Goodbye then.

[Silence.]

MIRIAM: Well kiss 'er goodbye, you daft ol' pig's bladder.

ZAC: Aye. Goodbye.

[Exit Gill.]

MIRIAM: Well don't just stand there like a lovesick goat, get on the path.

ZAC: There's summat I want to say first.

MIRIAM: What?

ZAC: About Gill. Last night.

MIRIAM: I don't want to know.

ZAC: What don't you want to know?

MIRIAM: About what happened.

ZAC: Nothing happened.

MIRIAM: I knows. *[pause]* I knows that.

ZAC: Well then, dear wife, which way shall us go? That way across the bog, or this way down the path?

[She kicks him.]

ZAC: What was that for?

MIRIAM: Everything. Get on with ee.

[The walk. Wind. They are back at camp.]

MIRIAM: There's still some life under the ashes 'ere.

ZAC: Good.

MIRIAM: Are the sheep all counted for?

ZAC: Forty-eight, an' pleased to see us an' all.

MIRIAM: Bring the child near the fire. I'll take him.

ZAC: I give thanks that you, an' the child, be still alive.

MIRIAM: Aye.

ZAC: I knows not what come over the world or what to do about it. I know not.

[Silence.]

Nor what stroke of fate it were that saved our child and not another.

MIRIAM: He lives because I bought his life with gold. I got the gold in exchange for the myrrh. You stole the myrrh from a king. 'Tis all of this world, Zac. An' yet I wouldn't say there weren't a drop o' luck in it.

ZAC: Luck? I call it more than luck.

MIRIAM: Call it what you may, he is alive — he is alive.

[The look at the baby together.]

ZAC: Miriam, what say you to this. We take the sheep to 'Ereford, an' sell 'em up. If I offers my service as head shepherd, I'll soon 'ave work, an' a roof over our heads. A fire, a bed, sheets — King and Queen?

MIRIAM: Why?

ZAC: I should never 'ave brought ee up 'ere. I see it now, how come I didn't see it before I can't tell, but I see it now.

MIRIAM: *[smiles]* 'Tis good thinking, Zac. 'Tis good.

ZAC: There is one condition.

MIRIAM: I'll have no conditions.

ZAC: You must stop kicking me.

MIRIAM: Bah — I never kicked ee 'ard.

ZAC: Hard as Hell an' always in the same place.

MIRIAM: Don't shout, you'll wake the baby. *[pause]* 'Tis a wonder ee 'ave slept through these two nights without waking once.

ZAC: Aye, he is a model baby. *[pause]*

We should find a name for the boy, lest we should both fall over a cliff and he be left nameless.

MIRIAM: *[puzzled]* What cliff?

ZAC: Any cliff. I was merely....

MIRIAM: There are no cliffs.

ZAC: You be so literal, Miriam. I meant no cliff that is real.

MIRIAM: No real cliff?

ZAC: Forget I ever mentioned a cliff.

MIRIAM: I shall. I have. It is forgotten. You an' yer imaginary cliffs.

[Silence.]

Now we 'ave stopped walking I am bitter cold again.

ZAC: Huddle up then.

MIRIAM: Get off.

ZAC: Sheep do huddle together to keep warm, so must we.

MIRIAM: I don't want to be anywhere near when you sell those sheep. You'll be all weeping and wailing.

ZAC: Aye. Look at them stars, Miriam. Do you see them stars?

MIRIAM: How can I not see them?

ZAC: Doesn't it fill ee with wonder and humility.

MIRIAM: Well aye. "Wonder" anyhow.

ZAC: See that. They calls that the Plough.

MIRIAM: Aye, you 'ave said so before.

ZAC: Though it looks more like a saucepan to me.

MIRIAM: 'Tis a perfect plough, Zac.

ZAC: Saucepan.

MIRIAM: Plough.

ZAC: Saucepan.

MIRIAM: Go to sleep, you daft ol' piece o' leather.

[Reprise of 'In The Bleak Midwinter'. At the end of the song, Miriam glances up at the stars.]

THE END

The Author

Charles Way was born in Devon in 1955. He trained as an actor at Rose Bruford College in London then joined Leeds Education team for whom he wrote his first professional play in 1978. He then became resident writer at Theatre Centre in London and has since written over thirty plays, many especially for young people. His plays include *The Flood,* (published by Collins), *Witness,* (Duke Playhouse, Lancaster), *She Scored For Wales* and *In living Memory* (Gwent Theatre). Adaptations include *On The Black Hill,* (Made in Wales) and *Ash On A Young Man's Sleeve,* (Sherman Theatre, Cardiff). *The Flood* and his version of *Sleeping Beauty* are both in production in Russia.

Charles has also written several large-scale community projects including the opera, *A Song of Streets,* for the Welsh National Opera and the people of Cardiff and *Bordertown* for Monmouth. Currently in production in Wales are *The Search for Odysseus,* (Made in Wales) and *Ill Met by Moonlight,* (Hijinx Theatre).

Note To The Series

Welsh drama found a new and distinctive voice in the eighties. Before that, there were new theatres in Wales, but there was little new drama. Why was it that there was a surge of new writing at this time? Perhaps it is no accident that the decade was one of economic hardship and unemployment. It would not be the first time that adversity has brought the best out of the Welsh. We can be certain, however, that new writers were sustained by the commitment of a band of theatre professionals, many of whom shared with them a common background and experience. During this period, new writers have been specifically fostered by the Made in Wales Stage Company. This academy of stage writing has had a crucial training role, enabling emerging dramatists to learn through workshops and the experience of seeing their plays performed in front of an audience. Other companies, such as Hijinx, The Sherman Theatre, Theatre Clwyd, Moving Being, Y Cwmni, and others, have commissioned new plays and/or taken them to community venues to people who would normally find theatres alien and intimidating. Welsh dramatists have benefited directly from this professional support system and indirectly from the patronage of public bodies but they have not yet reached the audiences that they deserve. Irish theatre-goers have in the past greeted new writers with riots, and today they still provide the oxygen of controversy, but if the attendance at some Welsh premieres is any indication, innovation in Wales meets with indifference from the public at large.

Seren, with the support of the Arts Council of Wales, are pleased to publish a series of new plays which will facilitate re-staging, enhance the status of new dramatists, and, we hope, help draw new audiences into our theatres. We cannot afford, nor would it be proper, to limit support to a movement or faction, if any exists. To the list of writers who were born in Wales, or who now live here, we will add the name of any writer of quality, who makes his or her initial breakthrough before Welsh audiences.

There are a number of questions that need to be answered about the present state of our theatre. Just how good are our writers? Is the neglect of English managements evidence of discrimination, or merely of lack of knowledge? Are we at last beginning to create a national theatre that will one day equal those of Scotland and Ireland? We hope that the publication of this drama series will help to find the answers.

Brian Mitchell
Editor